SHORT CIRCUITS

APHORISMS, FRAGMENTS, AND LITERARY ANOMALIES

EDITED BY

JAMES LOUGH

AND

ALEX STEIN

schaffner
press

SCHAFFNER PRESS
TUCSON ARIZONA

The editors are grateful to the following publishers for granting permission to
reprint from the works of the contributors to *Short Circuits*: Black Ocean,
Essay Press, Farrar Straus and Giroux, Graywolf Press, Grove Atlantic,
HarperCollins Publishers, Kelsey Street Press, Mekko Productions, Punctum
Books, Random House, St. Martin's Press, W.W. Norton, Wave Books,
White Pines Press, The American Poetry Review, Hotel Amerika, Interim,
Menage, Life and Legends, ECW Press, and Electric Literature.

For permission to reprint, contact:
Attn: Permissions
Schaffner Press
POB 41567
Tucson, Az 85717

First Paperback Edition: 2018

Cover and Interior Design: Jordan Wannemacher

For Library of Congress Copyright-in-Publication Information,
contact the Publisher.

ISBN: 978-1-943156-37-5
PDF: 978-1-943156-38-2
EPUB: 978-1-943156-39-9
MOBI: 978-1-9431256-40-

CONTENTS

INTRODUCTION BY JAMES LOUGH   5
PREFACE BY ALEX STEIN   27

JAMES RICHARDSON	31	ALEX STEIN	103
LYDIA DAVIS	37	DINTY W. MOORE	107
ALAIN DE BOTTON	41	H. L. HIX	117
CLAUDIA RANKINE	47	MICHAEL MARTONE	125
CHARLES SIMIC	51	ANA MARIA SHUA	129
JANE HIRSHFIELD	59	ERIC JAROSINSKI	139
JOY HARJO	61	GEORGE MURRAY	145
SARAH MANGUSO	65	YAHIA LABABIDI	151
MAGGIE NELSON	69	ELISA GABBERT	155
KARL JIRGENS	75	STEPHEN DOBYNS	161
DON PATERSON	79	DANIEL LIEBERT	173
CHARLES BERNSTEIN	89	MARGARET CHULA	181
SHARON DOLIN	97	MICHAEL THEUNE	
GEMMA GORJA	101	& AUSTIN SMITH	185

DAVID LAZAR	189
SAMI FEIRING	193
AARON HASPEL	197
S.D. CHROSTOWSKA	203
RICHARD KOSTELANETZ	209
LILY AKERMAN	215
JOSÉ ANGEL ARAGUZ	219
ASHLEIGH BRILLIANT	227
IRENA KARAFILLY	233
PATRICK CARR & CLAYTON LAMAR	239
HART POMERANTZ	245
MEG POKRASS	249
ERIC NELSON	253
HOLLY WOODWARD	259
MARTY RUBIN	261
MIKE GINN	265
JAMES GUIDA	271
DENISE HAYES	275
DR. MARDY GROTHE	281
OLIVIA DRESHER	287
JAMES LOUGH	293
LANCE LARSEN	299
ISAAC FELLOWS	303
WILLIAM PANNAPACKER	307
KARL KEMPTON	311
CHARLENE DEGUZMAN	317
PAUL PORTUGÉS	321
JOHN BRADLEY	325
TOM FARBER	329
KEVIN GRIFFITH	333
STEVEN CARTER	339
BRIAN JAY STANLEY	343
BHANU KAPIL	347
EMILY PECK	355
ZARA BELL	359
CONTRIBUTORS	363

THIS IS YOUR BRAIN ON WORDS

THE NEUROLOGICAL FRUITS
OF LITERARY SURPRISE

JAMES LOUGH

WORDS, LIKE DRUGS, change consciousness. One compliment can change a shirt you're not fond of into your favorite. One put-down can ruin a day. Whether spoken or written down, words act like psychoactive chemicals, altering our moods and outlooks, our opinions, doubts, and beliefs. And over the last twenty-five years, as words have started to reach us differently, namely via new media like the Internet, an effect has been the creation of ever more succinct written forms: tweets, Facebook posts, comment forums, and shrinking news stories, if we bother to read beyond the headlines.

One side effect is the complaint that even avid readers are now having trouble concentrating on long blocks of text. Assaulted by a variety of transient digital forms, the reading experience has gotten choppier, more distracted than focused, more associative than linear. This book, featuring only the shortest literary forms, can be seen as a brick and mortar adaptation to digital trends. But there is nothing new about the extremely short forms condensed into this book. Aphorisms go back at least 5000 years. Flash fiction—only a page or two in length—was not uncommon during the 12th century, the era of Chaucer and Boccaccio. And micro-essays—from a paragraph to a page long—have existed at least since Balthazar Gracian, in the 1600s, took Montaigne's invention from a century before, the personal essay, and boiled it down to a single paragraph. Even shorter forms like haiku date back at least as far as the 1600s, and people still write them. As ancient as they are, all of these forms still flourish, especially on the Internet, and they demand roughly the same attention span as a Facebook post or a *BuzzFeed* blurb. Ancient, we might say, is the new modern. It's nearly impossible to mention aphorisms anymore without someone bringing up Twitter. The social media platform that straitjackets writers into concision has mushroomed into a favored mode of expression for poets, philosophers, and even presidents.

Are writers of extremely short forms, in creating these weapons of mass distraction, only reinforcing readers' short attention spans? Quite possibly. But there are obvious differences. A steady diet of *BuzzFeed* is a far cry from a diet of Buddhist quotations. A self-respecting writer, feeding readers in very small bites, knows it helps to spice them with wit, insight, beauty, or surprise.

In *Short Flights*, the 2015 precursor to this volume, we spotlighted only aphorisms. This time around, we're using a floodlight to illuminate a more expansive mosaic of extremely short work that writers are playing with today: haiku, flash fiction, micro-essays, satiric dictionary entries, journal fragments, radically short poems, death poems, visual poems and mathematical poems. They all differ from aphorisms in intention and aesthetic effect—perhaps they share only brevity in common. But brevity is itself both an aesthetic statement and a philosophical stance: *less is more; don't waste words; get in and out quickly; brevity is the soul of wit.*

Literary works this short tend to deliver only a single, unified effect. Unlike longer works—short stories, long poems, novels, movie scripts—which carry a reader through multiple moods, ideas and perspectives, a very short work creates one intense sensation: one sharp feeling, one startling thought, one idol smashed, one prejudice uprooted and displayed for examination. What they sacrifice in duration, they make up for in exhilaration. Even when we read longer works, it is often the short utterances that penetrate us most deeply. The moments we remember most vividly from a novel, story, or long poem are just that—moments—a line or two: *It was the best of times; it was the worst of times; Her voice is full of money; It is a truth universally acknowledged, that a single man in possession of a good fortune, must be in want of a wife.* So, in this anthology we have gathered a collection of intense moments—emotional, conceptual, imaginative, mundane, and sublime. If words are drugs, then aphorisms, microfictions, mini-essays, and nano-poems are their delivery devices. A little later in this essay, we'll explore the very real and measurable effects these devices have upon our brains. But first, let's look at the literary forms on display in our pharmacopeia.

APHORISMS

Because of the Internet, those slim little sentences, aphorisms, that comprise the bulk of this book, have only multiplied in influence. One could argue that the aphorisms are the most *formal* form of very short writing, though haiku compete for this distinction. Writers cram a lot of mental and verbal craft into an aphorism, which by definition must be tiny and tidy. The best ones combine philosophical penetration, verbal compression, and sharp, ironic wit. Another quality readers expect from highly crafted aphorisms is surprise. As aphorism authority James Geary has put it, in his Five Rules for Aphorisms, an aphorism must have a twist.[1] It must lead the reader down one path then quickly switch to another.

I can resist anything except temptation.
OSCAR WILDE

It should sneak up behind readers' expectations and startle them, producing a spontaneous rush of suspension and delight. Later, we'll explore the paradoxical process writers undergo when engineering spontaneity into language.

HAIKU

The haiku may be the short form most readers have read or been arm-twisted into composing in grade school. Most of us are familiar with the rigid recipe—count the syllables, use plain language, throw in a visual image, imply season and setting, reflect on traditional themes. All these rules would seem to mock another precept, that the haiku must come to the poet spontaneously, depicting "a moment seized upon," as poet Robert Hass put it[2]. If it all comes together, the writer's insight and the poem's visual image fuse to trigger the haiku's single effect—a pang of feeling in the reader. In this volume, the haiku of Margaret Chula follow the traditional rules. But their themes often express a strikingly modern sense of hollow helplessness:

> *restless autumn sea*
> *remnants of Fukushima*
> *arrive at our shores*

Related to haiku are traditional Japanese death poems, influenced by Zen, in which poets who are near death share their final perceptions. Michael Theune and Austin Smith have collaborated to create the poignant, occasionally mordant, death poems included here, despite the fact that neither writer, we can hope, is at death's door.

MICROFICTION

Ernest Hemingway[3] has shown us what a fiction writer can accomplish in six words:

> *For sale: baby shoes, never worn.*

Microfiction, or flash fiction, is one of the longer short forms. Out in the world, the conventional word limits for flash fiction, or microfiction, can start around six words, or around 140 spaces (in the case of Twitterature), and can swell all the way up to four pages, which is far too longwinded for this collection. We settled on a rough maximum of four sentences, sometimes as many as six. The radically short stories by Lydia Davis, Ana Maria Shua, and Isaac Fellows show how extremely short stories, condensed into a few lines, can convey radically different sensibilities. Davis's present the viewpoint of a droll, painfully observant New Englander confronting an everyday world packed with ironies. Shua's stories are so light and dreamlike they might lift from the page on butterfly wings. Fellows' are enigmatic, Zen-like parables, which read like absurdist koans. Such a wide range of creative perception expressed in such tight quarters demonstrates how a humble hut made of words can contain many mansions.

MINI-ESSAYS

Once, at a bookstore reading for our earlier anthology *Short Flights*, we casually tossed out a request to the audience for alternative names for this genre, and the writer Kathryn T.S. Bass instantly offered, "Paragraphorisms!" We hope the label sticks. But for now, we'll stick to the conventional term mini-essay, a genre that is itself wide enough to accommodate the socially-conscious mini-memoirs by Claudia Rankine, the acute personal observations like those of Sarah Manguso and Maggie Nelson, or the dollhouse-scaled arguments by Elisa Gabbert. Mini-essays present nonfiction prose in a nutshell, insight layered upon insight in dialectical zigzags. Like microfictions, mini-essays tell a story. Their characters are not people but ideas, and their plots follow the paths that thought takes, switching back and forth toward some resolution, or irresolution.

MICRO-POEMS

Micro-poems are not new. In 1913, Ezra Pound showed us what poets could achieve in small spaces with visual images:

"In a Station of the Metro"
The apparition of these faces in a crowd;
petals on a wet, black bough.

Nearly a century before, Emily Dickinson routinely distilled poems to their essence in tiny, vibrant works like this one, about a hummingbird.

A route of evanescence
With a revolving wheel;
A resonance of emerald,
A rush of cochineal.

It seems there will always be a place in culture for extremely condensed poems. In these pages, Jane Hirshfield's short poems combine a Zen awareness with a poet's passion for language that sings. Eric Nelson's poems come about as close to aphorisms as possible while remaining poems. But, unlike a prose writer, a poet cannot abide line breaks determined by a typesetter. In Nelson's brief introduction to his poems, he demonstrates how the effect of his verse turns on its timing, and its timing on the break in the line.

SEQUENCES

Sharon Dolin, Alex Stein, Maggie Nelson, and Claudia Rankine stack short works in sequences that add up to longer works. Each aphorism or micro-essay in a sequence stands on its own as a discrete work; it could be lifted from its sequence and still feel complete. But in sequences, the linked works also serve the larger purpose of creating a larger, sustained work revolving around a cluster of ideas and aesthetic effects. The result is a montage of moments. In Rankine's sequence of mini-memoirs, a series of anecdotes that depict unconscious racism accumulate to create a sense of lasting outrage and exhaustion. Dolin uses the conceit of "the last aphorism," in which the writer works toward a paradoxical goal: compressing "truth into a pistachio nut" while writing to empty the meaning out of language and the "I" out of the writer. The result is a complex felt sense of ambition, nostalgia, and loss.

JOKES

In *Short Flights*, Hart Pomerantz defined aphorisms as "jokes that went to college." Beyond being short, jokes and aphorisms share other formal qualities. Obviously, both are succinct word constructions aiming to create a single, humorous effect (jokes) or a single, insightful point (aphorisms). But aphorisms are sometimes funny, and jokes can be insightful. So why are they considered different forms? Is it possible that the only significant difference between jokes and aphorisms is a difference of topic? Aphorisms tend to take on deeper philosophical, political, or social topics than jokes do, which would support Pomerantz's definition. The Twitter pieces included here by comedians Charlene deGuzman, Mike Ginn, Patrick Carr and Clayton Lamar ring like one-liners from standup. Yet some of these "jokes" also happen to address history, politics, and philosophy. Does that make them aphorisms, or at least aphoristic? Critics might respond that it's not the topic, but the language—more formal diction—that elevates aphorisms above jokes. But many of the aphorisms in this collection, including those by celebrated literary aphorists like James Richardson, partake in dark humor and don't use elevated diction. Compare his aphorisms to Rodney Dangerfield's joke about reincarnation:

It takes more than one life to be sure what's killing you.

In full disclosure, I just pulled a cheap trick. The aphorism above was written by Richardson, not Dangerfield. But is it beyond a reasonable doubt that Dangerfield could have written it?

One difference between jokes and aphorisms might have to do with whether either one upholds a consensus worldview or questions it. Is the author's persona sitting on the fringes of society, expressing an outsider's view? Or is she commenting from an overstuffed chair situated comfortably within social convention and expressing something funny, but which doesn't challenge traditional pieties. In the terminology of classical satire, is she Juvenalian (viciously incisive, subversive, finger-pointing) or Horatian (avuncular, winking, finger-wagging with a knowing smirk)? Both jokes and aphorisms can perform either function. Freud remarked on the uncanny power of jokes to undermine social conventions. All of which leaves me wondering if finding sharp distinctions between jokes and aphorisms is worth the strain. Ultimately, I find it more interesting to focus on what these little nuggets *do*, rather than what to call them. I'll leave it to others to codify what gets to be an aphorism, and what has to be a joke.

VISUAL (OR CONCRETE) POETRY

Visual poetry happens when a poet or visual artist uses words to create visual art. An elementary example would be a tree-shaped poem about a tree, but modern concrete poems are vastly more sophisticated. Some concrete poets deliberately strip the meanings from the words, using them only as visual elements. In this collection, however, we have favored writers who, in making their visual/verbal constructions, use denotative language to detonate fresh meanings. Some concrete poems are one-offs, visual puns or jokes. Others, like those of Karl Jirgens, resemble word puzzles. Richard Kostelanetz's picture poems present self-referential visual paradoxes that will also look good hanging over your sofa. Karl Kempton's word diagrams compress verbal concepts, creating double and even triple connotations. And while Paul Portuges's poems aren't technically visual poems, their structure, words falling like rain, influence how we collect their meaning.

LITERARY PERSONAE

The final aspect I'd like to draw attention to in this volume has little to do with length or form, but with the *personae*, or masks, writers might wear when composing them. Writers wear masks to free themselves from the exhausting slog of being themselves, as a ventriloquist might use a dummy to give voice to statements the ventriloquist (or the audience) might find uncomfortable or inappropriate. In a similar vein, playwrights use characters to express viewpoints that they themselves may or may not share. Shakespeare, for example, never makes a definitive point, but lets his characters revel in their own witty observations. A satirist like Jonathan Swift might disguise his identity to make provocative political points and incite action. In these pages, most of the "personae" aphorisms originated as Tweets. William Pannapacker's dark, hilarious observations of American culture were originally tweeted by "Werner Twertzog" (@WernerTwertzog), a fabricated, self-aggrandizing doppelganger of German filmmaker Werner Herzog. In July 2016, *Wired* magazine blew Pannapacker's cover in an article about the actual Herzog. Also included are Patrick Carr and Clayton Lamar, the writers behind @dogsdoingthings, in which dogs deliver mordant commentary on a meaning-challenged existence. In their case, the persona isn't precisely that of the dogs themselves, but of someone observing the dogs observing the world. And one could argue that Michael Theune and Austin Smith, contemporary Americans writing traditional Japanese death poems, are assuming the persona of an anonymous poet teetering at death's door.

FEED YOUR HEAD: LITERATURE IS "GOOD FOR YOU"

But let's return to words as drugs. In the past few years, psychologists have shown that reading literary works both short and long has benefits beyond instruction and delight. Committed readers of literary works probably don't need reminding, but occasional readers, reluctant readers, and non-readers may give reading a doubletake. As the worldviews of science and technology so permeate our daily lives, even those of us who do value sitting down with a book may find ourselves feeling defensive about our low-tech passion. If the 20th century produced a literature of anxiety, the 21st is anxious about literature. When pitted against glowing digital click bait, black words on a white page may seem primeval to those weaned on screens.

The good news—and ironic—is that the very technology that may seem to threaten literature is, in fact, affirming the profound ways that reading literature is uniquely vital to our minds and our lives. Bookish folks no longer need to make vague claims about the metaphysical values of reading. Science is reaffirming that language and literature are powerful technologies, linguistic brain gadgets working small miracles upon our minds. It has now been confirmed by brain science and cognitive psychology: words change consciousness and thus change lives.

Let me confess that I bridle at blunt scientific reductionism. I chafe against a worldview that boils down the complex interplay of readers and texts to a cluster of excitable cells firing in a three-pound blob of watery fat. And since the rise of functional magnetic resonance imaging (fMRI), such neural reductionism has been rampant. The temptation of brain science is to conflate correlation with causation: because the rooster crowed at five a.m., and then the sun rose, the sun rose because the rooster crowed. Or if, when strapped into an fMRI machine, our amygdala lights up while we think happy thoughts, we conclude, naturally, that we are happy *because* our amygdala lit up. Reducing human behavior to brain activity ignores the tremendous influences of family, education, culture, society, economics, and history—all of which, according to the reductionists, would seem to blanch before the awesome power of the Great White Brain. But the opposite is also true. Cultural determinists seem determined to ignore genetics and biology. But the brain/behavior correlation matters deeply. If the brains of a wide spectrum of people respond similarly to the same stimuli, this knowledge is not only meaningful. It is important for literature. In recent years, MRI studies have collected evidence that supports what book lovers have intuited for centuries. Far from being a threat to literature, brain science is revealing itself to be its powerful ally.

Let's start with how readers' brains benefit from long works like novels. Cognitive scientists have documented the benefits of reading character-driven novels, as opposed to plot-driven potboilers or to nonfiction. Readers who regularly read quality fiction, long stories that embroil them in the perspectives, daily lives, dilemmas, and relationships of fictional characters, are actually more empathetic than people who don't. Emanuele Castano and David Kidd at the New School for Social Research asked readers, after reading literary fiction, in this case *The Round House* by Louise Erdrich, to take tests measuring "their ability to infer and understand other people's thoughts and emotions"[4] They performed far better than those who had read a pop potboiler, *The Sins of the Mother* by Danielle Steele, or those who read a work of nonfiction.

It's easier for readers of serious fiction to walk in other people's shoes, feeling their feelings and predicaments as they feel their own. Reading about imaginary people makes real people more real and diminishes the otherness of "the other." In a world fraught with seemingly willful misunderstanding and conflict, few abilities seem more urgently needed than empathy. Think about it—transforming a person who does not feel for another person into one who does has been a goal of philosophers and religious figures for centuries, and more recently the goal of psychologists. And it turns out that exposure to a novel, a literary technology invented in the 16th century, will do the job nicely. This is little short of miraculous. And novels cost less than therapists.

If a long work like a literary novel can immerse us in a seamless dream and instill in us some fellow feeling, then what benefits can we reap from a very short work like an aphorism, a haiku or a piece of micro-prose? The benefits are different from those delivered by long works but equally profound. A short work can awaken us from our conditioning, the waking dream of ordinary life. This insight runs against the grain of postmodern thinking that has dominated literary scholarship since the publication of Jen-Francois Lyotard's book *The Postmodern Condition* (1984). Lyotard's prescription, "No grand narratives," tagged the aphorism as a suspect form. Aphorisms, the theory goes, assert general, "totalizing" statements, big claims to truth and authority that can't possibly be true for everyone. But what if we reframed the aphorism? What if we saw aphorisms as propositions, not conclusions, as forms that open discourse rather than resolving it? If someone disagrees with an aphorism's claim, let the ensuing dialogue explore its flaws. Debate, it would seem, is preferable to censorship.

Even so, certainty of any kind is dangerous, not only in political arenas, but also to our individual psyches. Certainty constrains our openness to experience, and our interpretations of experience, by locking us inside what behavioral scientists call cognitive biases, patterns of thinking in which we're certain something is true when in fact it may or may not be. These biases are everyday delusions, big and small. They are also common—we carry whole baskets of them. At times a bias can even be useful. If we are biased by the knowledge that there are bluebirds in these woods, that expectation can sharpen our attention, making us more likely to actually spot bluebirds. But cognitive biases can easily calcify into harmful cognitive states: mental sets. Mental sets are the conceptual ruts in which our thoughts run. They prevent us from seeing situations freshly or from alternative points of view. Mental sets—Blake's "mind forg'd manacles"—contribute to cognitive bias, which in turn reinforces mental sets. This process shackles creativity and closes minds. It's like the uncle who endlessly spouts the same adage "Early to bed, early to rise . . .," ignoring people who work best late at night. Even worse, mental sets can deal in stereotypes, reducing human beings to cartoon characters. The bad news is that mental sets are exasperatingly hard to avoid. For example, see if you can find a shape in this:

Once you've identified the shape, see if you can look again and *not* see it as a horse, or a dinosaur, or a dragon, but simply a random scribble. It's

IMAGE BY FRANK DIXON

next to impossible. Something in our minds wants to be sure and aches to be in control. Cognitive scientist Vera Tobin calls cognitive bias the "curse of knowledge," adding that "a pervasive cognitive bias…makes it very difficult for us accurately to imagine, once we know something, what it is like not to know it."[5]

Aphorisms, to some critics, harden into mental sets. But I would argue that aphorisms contain an element that not only diminishes mental sets but thoroughly deconstructs them: the element of surprise.

THE POETICS OF SURPRISE

Surprise is nothing new in literary works or films. In long work such as a novel, surprise can come with a plot twist. It can come in a movie like *The Crying Game*, when Dil reveals herself to be biologically male. Or in *The Usual Suspects*, when we learn that the diffident nebbish Verbal Kint is the mysterious sociopathic criminal Keyzer Sose. It can come in a mystery novel, when the character you least suspected turns out to be a hardened killer. Such surprises in long works can delight audiences and send them working backward through the plot to rediscover moments that hinted at, predicted, or in screenwriter's terminology, *motivated* the surprise. These versions of the "bait and switch" technique usually happen after extended baiting (roughly 1/3 of a screenplay's length in "plot points," or nearly the entire mystery novel) followed by a sudden switch that prompts the reader to see everything preceding that surprise in a new light.

In an aphorism, the surprise or twist happens after a "baiting" period that lasts only the better part of a sentence. Unlike the surprises found in a long work, aphoristic surprise does not throw everything that happened before the surprise into a new light. It throws readers back upon themselves, upon their own assumptions and expectations, and even on the startling way in which the aphorism manages to subvert them. Readers of aphorisms do not refer back to earlier moments in the text, but to earlier instances within themselves. In this sense, aphorisms are neither totalizing nor con-servative, preserving old conceptual wine bottles. They are radical, deliberately pouring new wine into old bottles with the full expectation that they will burst.

For a split second, the surprised reader of an aphorism experiences a gap, a rush of unknowing. She is tossed briefly into stomach-lifting weightlessness, as when driving a car over a gentle swell in the road. This instance of unknowing, this gap of suspended belief, is the central feature of the aphorism's "poetics of surprise."

On a personal note, I experienced a surprise in my research about writing and consciousness. I have long struggled to reconcile my writing vocation and my interest in contemplative practices like meditation. Could writing itself be turned into a contemplative practice that led to verifiable psychological, spiritual, and neurological results? I always came up empty. Meditation teachers J.K. Krishnamurti and Adi Da have both alluded to the salutary effect of using writing as a practice to slow one's thoughts, but I couldn't duplicate it.

The wall I always hit was that writing's raw material, language, is inherently dualistic. With words, it takes two to Tango. As products of discursive thought, words are understood in binary relation to the actual things (objects, concepts) they represent. Or, we understand words in relation to other words. Meditative practices, however, aim at stepping back from discursive thought, at realizing the One that both precedes and transcends the Two, a process called nondualism. So language that depends on subject-object relations cannot even remotely describe what exists prior to, behind, and beyond subject and object. Because meditation aims at states of consciousness that move beyond language into pure perception, language, and the reflective thoughts that drive it, are only impediments. Throwing words at post-verbal consciousness is as effective as throwing snowballs at the sun.

Then I had my moment of surprise. I had it all backwards. I had been struggling to find a way for the act of writing to open up the writer's consciousness to more expanded awareness. But I realized that expanded states of consciousness change one's writing more dependably than writing changes one's consciousness. As Chekhov put it, "If you want to work on your art, work on your life." The chief beneficiary of a writer's expanded consciousness is not the writer. It's the reader. Writing may not be able to elevate consciousness, but reading can. It elevates through the element of surprise.

MIND THE GAP

At one level, an aphorism's surprise is merely structural—it comes when a sentence suddenly reverses direction. The surprise provokes a small startle reflex. But, as Christopher R. Miller puts it, small surprises can "ramify into sustained states, such as wonder, fear, or indignation."[6] An aphorism of deep insight, in addition to delivering a gap of mental suspension, saturates the gap as dye saturates cloth, with the idea or insight's unique "color". The surprise, more than just a knee-jerk response to an aphorism's construction, is also conceptual, semantic, or philosophical. The insight digs deeper than mere structural surprise can. Often, a new idea delivered by an aphorism yanks the readers' unquestioned beliefs out from under their feet, forcing them to question their own assumptions. The aesthetic surprise can be exhilarating. It can also be unsettling, or painful, or painfully enlightening.

Neuroscientist Andrew Newberg and his research partner Mark Robert Waldman have studied these little cognitive surprises, these "aha" moments like the ones aphorisms can deliver. Newberg calls them little enlightenments, or insights, as compared to the big "E" enlightenment of the sort that mystics, Buddhist masters and yogis refer to. Little "e" enlightenments aren't uncommon, but they perform an essential function. By forcing us out of our mental sets, they actually manage to separate us from ourselves. An "aha" moment creates a gap between our inner observer, the "I" we feel ourselves to be beneath our skin, and our inner processes: thoughts, memories, and feelings. This tiny split, this "ability to observe ourselves as being separate from our daily thoughts and feelings," is enormously important. Buddhists call it *detachment*. This kind of detachment is often misconstrued as being impassive, emotionally cold, poker-faced, cut off from people, events, or feelings—the opposite of empathetic. But Buddhist detachment is more like what happens when your foot pushes a car's clutch, which literally detaches, or creates a space, between the gears in the transmission. We still think and feel, but pushing the mental clutch helps pull our awareness back a bit to observe the gears of thought and feeling spinning in our minds. This disengaged awareness can spare us the emotional drama of taking our inner states too seriously, of just blurting our thoughts or acting out feelings in neurotic ways.

According to Newberg, this detachment, this result of repeated, small "aha" moments, actually rewires pathways in our brains and "improves our inner state of well-being and our ability to cooperate with others without conflict." Little surprises, like the ones very short literary works deliver, help us solve problems, short-circuit worries and fears, and elicit empathy for others, feeling peaceful, tolerant and open-minded.[7] Neurologically, these "aha" moments of deep insight come when activity in the frontal and parietal lobes decreases. These are the brain's control centers—some would say control freaks. Insight comes once we relinquish control and the activity in these centers slows down.

With insight comes creativity. A team of neuroscientists in China, led by Qingbai Zhao, set out to study whether written language could trigger "aha" moments by breaking readers out of their habitual mental sets. In this case, the written language came in the form of highly condensed riddles called *chengyu*. Chengyu riddles consist of four characters arranged ungrammatically. Solving a chengyu requires apprehending what the four characters combine to mean, but in a way that transcends the denotative meaning of each character. A correct answer to a chengyu is larger than the sum of its four parts. It's an answer that arrives by surprise. Zhao's team looked at two processes. First, the "aha" feeling, the breaking of habitual associations, or mental grooves: *this* always reminds me of *that*. Second, the formation of novel associations, or new grooves: *now* this reminds me of something *different*. Satisfactory responses to chengyu, like those to most riddles, require us to break free of mind-forg'd manacles.

Participants were placed in fMRI machines and shown a riddle. Then they were asked to choose between four solutions, one of which was a "normal," or conventional solution. This was called a *noninsight* solution.

Another solution, a "novel" or unconventional answer—one requiring creativity fused to an "aha" moment—was called an *insight* solution. The remaining two choices were random. The neuroscientists then studied brain scans of those who provided insight vs. noninsight solutions. Those who gave noninsight solutions showed no change in their brain activity during the scans. But those who produced insight solutions experienced "aha" moments during the study, and their brains reflected this. The hippocampus and amygdala regions, where surprise registers and novel associations are formed, lit up like a Christmas tree.[8]

It's not a stretch to assert that reading an aphorism, which can deliver a similar moment of suspended thought followed by a new realization—an "aha" moment—could induce similar brain changes. Aphorisms are cousins to riddles like chengyu. With a little sleight of pen, we can convert one into the other. Oedipus' riddle of the Sphinx . . .

What walks on four feet in the morning, two in the afternoon and three at night?

. . . can be turned into an aphorism.

A human walks on four feet in the morning, two in the afternoon, and three at night.

The aphoristic version still requires the reader to puzzle over the analogy and "solve" or comprehend it. The same goes for the following, an old Irish riddle:

What gets longer as you cut away at its end?

Can be "aphorized" as such:

One thing that gets longer as you chip away at its end—a grave.

Enough of these "aha" moments, these little "e" enlightenments, as Newberg calls them, may even accumulate into larger "E" experiences. Certain religious contemplatives are well aware of the connection between riddles, insight, and spirituality.

In his book *The Paradox of the Mystical Text*, Charles M. Jenkins, a scholar of medieval religious texts, cites how monastics in the Middle Ages used spiritual riddles to achieve at least an intellectual approximation to a mystical experience, Newberg and Waldman's small "e" enlightenments. Here's a medieval riddle:

On the way a miracle: water became bone.[9]

According to Jenkins, "The revelation of the riddle's secret, often found in a period of mental displacement which is similar to the mystical moment, is akin to the ecstasy felt by the mystic as a result of the revelations perceived during mystical experiences".

Jenkins doesn't go so far as saying that solving a riddle is the same as receiving a mystical experience. The small "e" enlightenment is a lesser sort…"the difference between discovering a spiritual mystery and the uncovering of an allegorical figure or the solving of a riddle are incomparable in intensity—since mystical ecstasy is more emotional than intellectual, more surprising, more sudden, more spontaneous, and more illuminating…"[10]

Other traditions are less cautious with the comparison. The Zen koan is an enigmatic riddle designed to throw aspirants' minds off their rails, collapsing their mental sets to reveal a larger, more capacious, blissful awareness behind, beneath, or prior to the mental set. This one is perhaps the most well known:

What is the sound of one hand clapping?

Or another, from *The Gateless Gate*, in which the Zen teacher invites a pupil to

Show me your Original Face, the face you had before your parents were born.

Koans promise more than just a junior varsity mystical experience. When a Zen student, under mind-numbing intellectual and emotional exertion, seemingly headed nowhere, suddenly "solves" a koan, the effect may start with a new intellectual awareness, but it can swiftly avalanche into a much deeper, more transformative experience of satori, or awakening to one's essence. So paradoxically, a language device can deliver an experience that transcends language. One cliché about mystical experiences is that words cannot describe them, and the ordinary, habituated mind cannot understand them. They reveal St. Paul's "peace of God, which passeth all understanding" (Philippians 4:7). But even if words aren't much use in describing expanded states of consciousness, if they feature the element of surprise, they can also trigger them.

I'll end this essay with the experience of a meditation teacher I have studied with, Gary Weber. He has a Ph.D. in materials science and has worked at executive levels in both corporate and government administration. His approach to contemplative techniques is pragmatic and empirical. He is also interested in how enlightenment experiences change the brain physically. Intriguingly, he had his first satori experience while reading a poem, one famous in the Zen tradition. In his words:

It was during graduate school, [I was] eating a bag lunch on the lawn of Old Main, the main admin building @ Penn State. I had just started on my search for a way to end my internal narrative, blah— blah.

I had found this book, bibliomantically, propitiously, in the university library, and when i read the first line "All beings are from the very beginning Buddhas" (in the translation I had), the entire world opened up into a space I hadn't even imagined could exist and remained so for 30 to 45 minutes. In addition to its transcendent and 'psychedelic' (I have never taken any) nature, was the clear seeing that there were no thoughts, only this great Stillness, which confirmed for me that it was possible to end the 'blah, blah'.

It was clearly the absolute truth, although I had no background in Buddhism or Zen. I didn't even know what this book was about until I looked at the cover and it said 'Zen,' so I started off finding some of these Zen folk to teach me how to reach that state again, and hopefully to remain there.

The poem was 'Song of Zazen' or 'Zazen Wasan.'[1] The content, and the poem, were actually totally relevant, as that is arguably the most famous poem in Zen, and, and I had just started on my search for a way to end my internal narrative, blah—blah.[11]

Weber had set out to get beyond language, the "blah blah" of internal narrative, and yet it was language, the Zen poem, that triggered his release from language. The first line of the poem, eight simple words, sent him into ecstatic rapture that transformed his life. Language can profoundly change brains and lives. Words act like consciousness-changing drugs, either for a little while or permanently. Contrary to the claims of linguistic determinism advanced by Nietzsche, by postmodernist theorists and by some linguists, language is not *only* a prison house. This idea, though most linguists have discredited it, still hangs on tenaciously in some literary circles. Despite the partial truth of the prison house metaphor—language as distorting mirror or mind forg'd manacle—certain types of language are actually capable of transporting us far beyond language.

If language is a prison house, then the key—also language—has been left in the lock.

NOTES

1. Geary, James. *The World in a Phrase: A Brief History of the Aphorism*. New York: Bloomsbury Publishing, 2005.

2. Hass, Robert, introduction to *The Essential Haiku: Versions of Basho, Buson, & Issa*. Ed. Robert Hass (Hopewell, New Jersey: The Ecco Press, 1994), xiv.

3. Whether Hemingway actually wrote this is a matter of dispute.

4. Chiaet, Julianne, "Novel Finding: Reading Literary Fiction Improves Empathy," *Scientific American*. Oct. 24, 2013.

5. Tobin, Vera, "Cognitive Bias and the Poetics of Surprise," *Language and Literature*, Vol 18(2): 155-172 doi: 10.1177/0963947009105342. www.sagepublications.com

6. Miller, Christopher R. *Surprise: The Poetics of the Unexpected from Milton to Austen*. Ithaca, NY: Cornell University, 2015, 4.

7. Newberg, Andrew M.D. and Mark Robert Waldman, *How Enlightenment Changes Your Brain*. (New York: Penguin-Avery, 2016), 19.

8. Zhao, Qingbai, Zhijin Zhao, Haibo Xu, Shi Chen, Fang Xu, Wenliang Fan, Lei Han. (2013) "Dynamic Neural Network of Insight: A Functional Magnetic Resonance Imaging Study on Solving Chinese 'Chengyu' Riddles," *PLoS ONE* 8(3): e59351.

9. https://doi.org/10.1371/journal.pone.0059351

10. Matterer, James L., "Riddles," Godecokery, http://www.godecookery.com/godeboke/godeboke.htm

11. Jenkins, Charles. *The Paradox of the Mystical Text*. Lewiston, NY: Edwin Mellen Press, 2003, 95-96.

12. Weber, Gary, Facebook message to author, December 14, 2016.

INFINITY IN THE PALM OF YOUR HAND

ALEX STEIN

INTEREST IN SMALLER forms—interest in the aphorism, yes, but interest, also, in ant farms, bee colonies, snowflakes (with their crystal-pattern revelations), psalms written on rice grains (I saw that once at The Ripley's Believe It or Not Museum in San Francisco), humming birds, haiku, and lonely, distant ideas.

A frog haiku—*The old pond. / A frog jumps in. / Splash!*—was said to have proved the enlightened state of the one (Basho) who wrote it.

In some translations, the word "Splash!" is replaced by the phrase, "the sound of thunder."

In case that helps.

⋮

The entirety of the apple tree, branches to roots, is contained in the apple seed.

⋮

Fallen petals—
the priest sweeps them
into the prayer room.

⋮

Why are some thoughts long and some short? One can ask the same question about icicles. Some icicles are long because they are long. Some icicles are short because they are short. Some thoughts, some loves, some lifetimes: short because they are short. While others go on and on.

⋮

Moonlight simplifies.
Sunlight clarifies.
Starlight multiplies.

⋮

It is the echo of small things, through the ages, across cultures, that carries the promise our humanity will overwhelm, in the end, our inhumanity. Basho's frog; the roar of a dandelion; the shadow of a floating seed. The tiny immutable memories of mountain crossings, and ocean crossings, in the depths of our ancestral minds.

The "self" is plural;
the "we" of our "I"
is silent.

⋮

But, think—if we did not contain multitudes, how would we bear the loneliness?

⋮

Short writing is capable of everything of which long writing is capable—except excess. Though, obviously, short writing is not, automatically, better than long writing, simply because it is shorter. Short writing is only better than long writing, if it is better, because it is better. Everything boils down to its essence. In short writing, nothing is abbreviated, that is the main thing to remember. Everything is still written out to its fullest extent. When a short writing is completed, there is nothing remaining to be told. Art seeks, or should seek, its irreducible minimum; the least that is still the necessary. Sometimes this means a novel. Sometimes it means a single dot, just off-center of an otherwise unmarked canvas.

⋮

"I want" is the beginning of "I am."

⋮

Complication is vanity.

⋮

The poet William Blake's lines—*To see the world in a grain of sand, / and heaven in a wild flower, / hold infinity in the palm of your hand, / and eternity in an hour*—are surely apropos.

Dear Reader: Welcome to *Short Circuits*.

JAMES RICHARDSON

Q: You work in both poetry and aphorisms. Presumably the two come from different mindsets—how do you decide whether a subject, or a state of mind, is better suited to a poem or an aphorism?

A: We all have strength enough to bear the troubles…of others.

La Rochefoucauld recalls truisms about life never giving us more than we can handle, but then (I add a stand-up comedian's pause) veers into something both darker and lighter. An aphorism, maybe, is a blend of proverb and joke. Porchia, too, starts on proverbially, on The Chosen Road of Life

> Before I traveled my way…I *was* my way.

But he deepens into something before and beyond choice. His twist isn't funny, but it shares with jokes a sensitivity to sequence. Punchline last, please.

> I traveled my way before I was my way

only flatly states a fact.

Aphorisms, that is, are re-definitions. In the greguería this is spectacularly obvious. "Milk is whipped sleep" (Ramón). But more frequently it's visible in twists, particularly in the repetition and re-seeing of a key word. "All work is the avoidance of harder work." The aphorist has the alert perversity of the punster, waiting for a word or idea to pressure, to mis-hear, to change. Looking for poems is the opposite: an unfocused gaze. James Merrill has likened it to fishing.

Short answer: one starts with a mindset, which is essentially a genre, rather than with a subject, and categorizing what results turns out to be much less of a problem than coming up with anything at all!

⋮

It takes more than one life to be sure what's killing you.

Worry wishes life were over.

Minds go from intuition to articulation to self-defense, which is what they die of.

I am saving good deeds to buy a great sin

Some things, like faith, cheer, courage, you can give when you do not have them.

Why should the whole lake have the same name?

How much less difficult life is when you do not want anything from people. And yet you owe it to them to want something.

If I can keep giving you what you want, I may not have to love you.

Idolaters of the great need to believe that what they love cannot fail them, adorers of camp, kitsch, trash that they cannot fail what they love.

No criticism so sharp as seeing they think you need to be flattered.

Time heals. By taking even more.

Competition and sympathy are joined at the root, as may be seen in the game *My grief is greater than yours,* which no one can keep himself from playing.

How fix the unhappy couple, when it was happiness they loved in each other?

After a while of losing you, I become the one who has lost you. Did the pain change me, or did I change to lessen the pain?

Experience tends to immunize against experience, which is why the most experienced are not the wisest.

The mind that's too sensitive feels mostly itself. A little hardness makes us softer for others.

You who have proved how much like me you are: how could I trust you?

Believe stupid praise, deserve stupid criticism.

I need a much larger vocabulary to talk to you than to talk to myself.

Determinism. How romantic to think the mind a machine reliable enough to transform the same causes over and over again into the same effects. When even toasters fail!

No use placing mystical trust in the body. It is perfectly adapted to life a million years ago. *Eat while you can, flee, strike.* But what does it know about cities, love, speculation? Nor will evolution change it, since failure now leads not to death and subtraction from the gene pool but merely to misery.

If I didn't have so much work to keep me from it, how would I know what I wanted to do?

It gets harder and harder to be free. Every time I need a larger labor to be at the end of.

While everyone clamored at the god, I kept aloof, scorning their selfishness. Now that he has ascended, I hate him because he does not guess what I want.

When you laughed at me, I could have been free, but instead of laughing with you, I clung to my imprisonment.

I could explain, but then you would understand my explanation, not what I said.

I keep glimpsing the loneliness I want, my thoughts without me.

The best disguise is the one everyone else is wearing.

Pleasure is for you. Joy is for itself.

The dead are still writing. Every morning, somewhere, is a line, a passage, a whole book you are sure wasn't there yesterday.

The happy and the suffering probably understand life equally well, but the sufferers may see a little more clearly how little it is that they understand.

Everywhere he looked Nerval saw a black spot. That one's easy, but where the optic nerve enters the retina there is another one, quite literally a blind spot. We never notice: the brain, like a mother softening the bad news, continually fills it in, never letting us know there is nothing there. O, spot I never see, from you I learn my landscapes are movies, my words a greeting card, my memories an official explanation!

LYDIA DAVIS

Q: Frequently, there is an element of surprise in your work, an unexpected response, an unforeseen coincidence, or an irony of circumstance. Do your stories ever surprise even you?

A: Sometimes a story is born of (inspired by) that surprise, unexpected coincidence, striking pattern of behavior or circumstance. In other cases, there is a sort of opening proposition in the story, which I then develop with only a rough or general idea of where it might go. Where it actually does go is always a surprise in its details, and sometimes also in its overall trajectory. I do think one has to be very open to what the less consciously controlled parts of the brain may suggest or even require. This is happening right now with a story I am in the early stages of. I was clear about the title and the general idea, but very quickly the nature of the story changed so that the title was no longer a good one. In this case, the title was a bit smart-alecky. But the story, and the main character, wanted to be more serious, more human, and the title in turn needed to be more subdued, more serious. One can absolutely never be rigidly faithful to one's first ideas, in the process of composition.

THE CORNMEAL

This morning, the bowl of hot cooked cornmeal, set under a transparent plate and left there, has covered the underside of the plate with droplets of condensation: it, too, is taking action in its own little way.

CAN'T AND WON'T

I was recently denied a writing prize because, they said, I was *lazy*. What they meant by *lazy* was that I used too many contractions: for instance, I would not write out in full the words *cannot* and *will not*, but instead contracted them to *can't* and *won't*.

THE LANGUAGE OF THE TELEPHONE COMPANY

"The trouble you reported recently is now working properly."

A WOMAN, THIRTY

A woman, thirty, does not want to leave her childhood home.

Why should I leave home? These are my parents. They love me. Why should I go marry some man who will argue and shout at me?

Still, the woman likes to undress in front of the window. She wishes some man would at least look at her.

JUDGMENT

Into how small a space the word *judgment* can be compressed: it must fit inside the brain of a ladybug as she, before my eyes, makes a decision.

SHORT CONVERSATION
(IN AIRPORT DEPARTURE LOUNGE)

"Is that a new sweater?" one woman asks another, a stranger, sitting next to her.

The other woman says it's not.

There is no further conversation.

MY CHILDHOOD FRIEND

Who is this old man walking along looking a little grim with a wool cap on his head?

But when I call out to him and he turns around, he doesn't know me at first, either—this old woman smiling foolishly at him in her winter coat.

OLD WOMAN, OLD FISH

The fish that has been sitting in my stomach all afternoon was so old by the time I cooked and ate it, no wonder I am uncomfortable—an old woman digesting an old fish.

ALAIN DE BOTTON

Q: Your longer nonfiction and fiction have a deeply humane and compassionate streak. Your aphorisms, though, tend to display a more satiric, ironic vision. What is it about the writing of aphorisms that changes a writer's point of view?

A: Aphorisms reward a clean upturning of an established truth. When one flips sentimentality, out comes cynicism.

⋮

Bitterness: anger that forgot where it came from.

Insomnia: the mind's revenge for all the thoughts you were careful not to have in the day.

The best cure for one's bad tendencies is to see them fully developed in someone else.

Mental health: having enough safe places in your mind for your thoughts to settle.

It takes a serious lack of imagination to have an entirely clean conscience.

A key goal of parenting: to try to ensure a child grows up with no wish to become famous.

The constant challenge of modern relationships: how to prove more interesting than the other's smartphone.

Tweets; to literature as Lego is to architecture.

The difference between bitterness, confusion, nostalgia—and resilience is...a plan.

Hope is a muscle—and like any muscle in constant use, needs rest.

Inviting someone to marry you may not be the kindest thing to do to someone you claim to love.

We don't fall in love with those who will make us happy so much as with those who feel familiar.

Anyone who isn't embarrassed of who they were last year/yesterday probably isn't learning enough.

Bookshops are the best destination for the lonely, given the numbers of books written because authors couldn't find anyone to talk to.

A strong desire not to be alone: a sure sign one is incubating a difficult message to tell oneself.

Marriage: to focus on the inherent difficulty of the project, not the alleged drawbacks of its participants.

Sustaining a relationship is largely about being disloyal to the Romantic emotions that got you into it.

Definition of a failure: someone who needs other people to fail.

The difference between hope and despair: a way of telling alternative stories from the same facts.

Most of what makes a book 'good' is that we are reading it at the right moment for us.

You have to be bashed about a bit by life to see the point of flowers, pretty skies and uneventful 'boring' days.

The internet is to this generation of writers as alcohol was to previous ones: anxiety suppressant, enemy of talent, challenge.

There are people we'd long ago have forgotten about if they hadn't started to ignore us.

There is no such thing as work-life balance. Everything worth fighting for unbalances your life.

Change begins when the fear of not acting at all at last outstrips the paralysing fear of making a mistake.

To stand any chance of choosing a partner wisely, it helps to be utterly reconciled to being alone all one's life.

Hypochondria: an above-average imagination applied to the deeply improbable nature of being alive.

An epidemic of loneliness is created by the misguided idea that the only cure to loneliness is a romantic relationship.

We believe we seek happiness in love, but what we may actually seek is familiarity—which can complicate any plans for happiness.

Two ways to feel more successful: achieve more. Or surround ourselves with people who have achieved less.

Wanting to be famous: an attempt to shortcut the arduous business of making friends.

For paranoia about 'what other people think': remember that only some hate, a very few love—and almost all just don't care.

The possession of a tortured soul is, sadly, simply no guarantee of also being a great artist.

The best way to be a calmer and nicer person is to give up on everyone, realising one simply is, where it counts, irredeemably alone.

Deep charm: despair lightly, humourously (non-accusingly) worn.

The cure for infatuation: get to know them better.

CLAUDIA RANKINE

Q: In *Citizen: An American Lyric*, you use multiple forms to make many points—long-form essay, micro-essay, personal anecdote, video script, poetry, photography, visual collage, itemized list. The forms accumulate into a montage of moments that distill the shattering experience of being black in the U.S.A. How did you arrive at this formal approach, as opposed to a more traditional book-length essay or collection of poems?

A: Muriel Rukeyser, in her poem "The Book of the Dead" includes twenty sections of testimony from Washington hearings, stock market reports, x-ray analysis, and letters. Regarding her formal break with lyric conventions, Rukeyser wrote, "I think very strongly that this is the material of poetry for us now, that it is our business to extend the document."

The activity of extending the document beyond the limit of its genre contains, in my view, contaminated fields of possibility (contaminated because the habits of that genre are disrupted and generative because the perceived sense of unity contained in the habits of that genre are disrupted). Reading, as defined by Juliana Spahr, in her "connective poetics," becomes "a negotiation rather than a conquering, an exchanging rather than a fixing," when one is willing to navigate the broken form.

⋮

At the end of a brief phone conversation, you tell the manager you are speaking with that you will come by his office to sign the form. When you arrive and announce yourself, he blurts out, I didn't know you were black!

I didn't mean to say that, he then says.

Aloud, you say.

What? He asks.

You didn't mean to say that aloud.

Your transaction goes swiftly after that.

And when the woman with multiple degrees says, I didn't know black women could get cancer, instinctively you take two steps back though all urgency leaves the possibility of any kind of relationship as you realize nowhere is where you will get from here.

A friend tells you he has seen a photograph of you on the Internet and he wants to know why you look so angry. You and the photographer chose the photograph he refers to because you both decided it looked the most relaxed. Do you look angry? You wouldn't have said so. Obviously this unsmiling image of you makes him uncomfortable, and he needs you to account for that.

If you were smiling, what would that tell him about your composure in his imagination?

Despite the fact that you have the same sabbatical schedule as everyone else, he says, you are always on sabbatical. You are friends so you respond, *easy*.

What do you mean?

Exactly, what do you mean?

Standing outside the conference room, unseen by the two men waiting for the others to arrive, you hear one say to the other that being around black people is like watching a foreign film without translation. Because you will spend the next two hours around the round table that makes conversing easier, you consider waiting a few minutes before entering the room.

The real estate woman, who didn't fathom she could have made an appointment to show her house to you, spends much of the walk-through telling your friend, repeatedly, how comfortable she feels around her. Neither you nor your friend bothers to ask who is making her feel uncomfortable.

To live through the days sometimes you moan like deer. Sometimes you sigh. The world says stop that. Another sigh. Another stop that. Moaning elicits laughter, sighing upsets. Perhaps each sigh is drawn into existence to pull in, pull under, who knows; truth be told, you could no more control those sighs than that which brings the sighs about.

The sigh is the pathway to breath; it allows breathing. That's just self-pres-ervation. No one fabricates that. You sit down, you sigh. You stand up, you sigh. The sighing is a worrying exhale of an ache. You wouldn't call it an illness; still it is not the iteration of a free being. What else to liken yourself to but an animal, the ruminant kind?

In line at the drugstore it's finally your turn, and then it's not as he walks in front of you and puts his things on the counter. The cashier says, Sir, she was next. When he turns to you he is truly surprised.

Oh, my God, I didn't see you.

You must be in a hurry, you offer.

No, no, no, I really didn't see you.

You wait at the bar of a restaurant for a friend, and a man, wanting to make conversation, nursing something, takes out his phone to show you a picture of his wife. You say, bride that she is, that she is beautiful. She is, he says, beautiful and black, like you.

When the waitress hands your friend the card she took from you, you laugh and ask what else her privilege gets her? Oh, my perfect life, she answers. Then you both are laughing so hard, everyone in the restaurant smiles.

Closed to traffic, the previously unexpressive street fills with small bodies. One father, having let go of his child's hand, stands on the steps of a building and watches. You can't tell which child is his, though you follow his gaze. It seems to belong to all the children as it envelops their play. You were about to enter your building, but do not want to leave the scope of his vigilance.

CHARLES SIMIC

SF: Many of your pieces here are lifted from journals, observations on unusual things you've seen in the course of a usual day. What can you tell us about the different aesthetic effect of such observations, on the one hand, versus the more carefully crafted aphorisms, on the other?

CS: I have never in my life attempted to write a "carefully drafted aphorism". My scribblings are just that—compulsive scribblings. I write down whatever pops into my head—something I've seen or remembered—into a notebook, on a scrap of paper, back of an envelope—and put it aside and don't look at it again for months or years. In other words, there's nothing deliberate about these creations, so when I find them, I'm as surprised by them as anyone else. Of course, I've tinkered with some of them a bit, but I'm careful not to overdo it. Whatever charm they have for me comes from their spontaneity.

SF: Your short works, aphorisms or fragmentary observations, sometimes display an awareness or an apprehension of a numinous aspect of life and art. Care to comment on that?

CS: I'm a New England Transcendentalist, born and raised in the Balkans, whose ancestors were Orthodox priests and whose father was a lifelong follower of Gurdjieff, the Russian mystic and spiritual teacher of Armenian and Greek descent who taught both in Paris and New York. Most of my adult life I spent teaching Emerson, Thoreau, Whitman and Dickinson, so all that stuff must have rubbed off on me. Since I don't believe in God or go to church, I'm always surprised that I have such strong religious feelings—but I do. Inevitably, I deal with the subject both in my poems and in my other writings.

⋮

He was writing a ballet for the radio, or did I hear it wrong in that noisy restaurant?

I keep a hoard of old watch faces in a drawer which I look at and touch from time to time.

"Jesus is a gun being fired" on the wall of a house trailer in Alabama.

Her life, she said, was an out-of-tune piano played by her various lovers.

This evening I sat listening to five presidential candidates offering their imaginary solutions for a country that doesn't exist.

"Imaginary maladies are much worse than the real ones, because they're incurable," an old friend who walks with difficulty was telling me.

"When Alfred snored he woke the dead." I'd like to see that on his gravestone.

Nudes in a museum give the impression that they like to be looked at both by lone men and by large groups of people. It's as if they stick their boobs out farther, let their fingers wander down to their crotches a bit more. Only the guards, I notice, keep their eyes lowered as if the women we are ogling are their wives and daughters.

There's nothing more boring in all of creation than a poet who tells the reader that he is using language to write his poems.

They gave the nice old gentleman I met at the bake sale several medals for the misery he caused in some country that no one could find any longer on the map.

He sat on a bench in Washington Square Park whispering something extremely confidential to his dog, who sat before him with ears perked, wagging his tail tentatively from time to time.

I once saw a man in full Indian costume, feathers and all, crossing 8th Avenue and 38th Street at five in the morning eating a slice of pizza.

The crosses all men and women must carry through life are even more visible on this dark and rainy November evening.

My life is as real as yours, said the cricket in the thicket as night fell.

Summer is no fun without sloth. Indolence requires patience—to lie in the sun, for instance, day after day—and I have none left. When I did, it was bliss. I lived like the old Greeks who knew nothing of hours, minutes, and seconds. No wonder they did so much thinking back then. When Socrates staggered home late after a day of philosophizing with Plato, his bad-tempered wife Xantippe could not point to a clock on the wall while chewing him out.

Two dogs, one jumping from the dock into the lake to retrieve the sticks his owner keeps throwing and the other one looking on in disgust.

"Can't you hear the rattling noise these snakes make as they crawl up the steps of the Capitol?" asked a homeless old woman squatting in a doorway in downtown Washington after I gave her a dollar.

For the sweet old couple working side by side in a garden, ignorance of what goes on in the rest of the world has been the secret of their lifelong happiness.

In the country, dark nights let themselves into our homes and make themselves comfortable as if they own the place.

I read somewhere that Napoleon, who feared neither the sword nor the bullet, was afraid of a dark room.

"A gentleman of the old school," people used to say about my father. Like his son, he used to wait for the leaves outside his window to fall asleep first before he himself did.

Cold December night. A homeless woman cowering in a doorway on East 3rd Street in New York talking to God, and he, tongue-tied as usual.

Gypsy fortune-teller sitting at a small round table in her parlor late one night and staring intently into an iPhone while waiting for a customer.

His was a sad, sad love story that made everyone who heard it laugh.

Every poet has his or her own way of mourning the passage of time. That may be the solution to the mystery of why so many people are drawn to poetry.

"I'd rather listen to a tree than to a philosopher," my old friend Tony Perniciaro used to say, but now the trees have no leaves and nothing to say to the snow just beginning to fall.

The sun shone this morning through the bare, astonished trees knee-deep in scarlet leaves, at a loss for what to do with all this fallen beauty.

Dark Night of the Soul theme park. St. John of the Cross hopping in and out of the woods chasing a firefly with a butterfly net.

While bombs fell on Belgrade, my aunt told me, she wished she had Clinton's number so she could plead with him to take it easy.

"I would have given my pants for…" my uncle kept shouting all his life.

Country roads lined with trees weary now of their leaves and fed up with chirping of their birds.

Night sky: Lights flashing on God's answering machine.

Two windows full of exotic flowers and palm trees. They live in a jungle, I conclude. They use a tiger for a sofa. Their children are little monkeys. When their mother walks in naked from the bath, the parrot in the cage shrieks, the father throws up his hands full of exotic butterflies.

At sunrise, there are windows that due to their privileged location on some high floor appear to be in a state of ecstasy.

This July afternoon, in the Central Park Zoo, I came across many animals as bored as I was.

God and Devil browsing side by side in a used bookstore.

A barber had a gun pointed at his head as he trimmed the moustache of a dictator.

I'm not who I think I am, you are not who you think you are, so who the hell are we then?

Prisoner of memories, I often find myself pacing inside one of their small cells.

There are two options for any small town dweller during dark months of the year: to die of boredom or become a philosopher.

JANE HIRSHFIELD

Q: What is your favorite contemporary very short poem? Who wrote it and what does it mean to you?

A: One short poem that is for me a north star of the possible is W.S. Merwin's:

> *"Elegy"*
> *who would I show it to.*

I can't think of a poem that carries more weight of meaning in so light a vessel. And for me, that is the essence of poetry: words that carry more than words alone can hold, that know more than words alone can know— yet do this by and with words. And by, and with, and from inside of, life, without which no word would have meaning.

This poem is a cupboard stripped bare, whose treasure is the wood of the cupboard. Within its seeming simplicity are basins and ranges, forests and rivers and glaciers, of loss, and of continuance, also. By its existence, the poem both sustains and disbands its own question. Its seven words (including the indispensable title) live in desolation, but also in desolation's after-world. The poem offers me promise, each time I have reason to go to it, that an after-world is possible, and that William Merwin unlocks for me one of its gates.

⋮

Sentence

The body of a starving horse cannot forget the size it was born to.

Maple

The lake scarlets
the same instant as the maple.
Let others try to say this is not passion.

Lemon

The grated lemon rind bitters the oil it steeps in.
A wanted flavor.
Like the moment in love when one lover knows
the other could do anything now wanted, yet does not.

Global Warming

When his ship first came to Australia,
Cook wrote, the natives
continued fishing, without looking up.
Unable, it seems, to fear what was too large to be comprehended.

To Sneezing

Pure master of all our losses,
dissolver of self and its zeals—
we bow before you as newspaper bows to the match.

JOY HARJO

Q: You have said "poetry came into the world with music" and that "most poetry isn't on the page." Can you expand on that, a little?

A: When you follow the roots of poetry, of any place, time or culture, the roots lead you back to the beginning. There you will find poetry hanging out with music and dance. They are inseparable. I followed the roots from the university, where I studied poetry in books, and wrote poetry that was published in magazines, anthologies and eventually books—back home to the Muscogee Creek Nation where I discovered a distant cousin on my father's mother's side, Alexander Posey, a very well-known poet in the late 1800's and early 1900's. He is still known in our tribal community for his poetry and for founding the first Native American daily newspaper in Eufaula, Oklahoma.

Following these roots led me to the ceremonial grounds, which is the heart of our traditional culture. Poetry is there in many forms. Poetry is in the song making its way around the fire with dancers, the rhythm kept by the shell shakers. Some of the finest poetry comes from those skillful in traditional oratory, Punvkv cvpkeckv. It is spoken in the Mvskoke language, in a kind of rhythm that's somewhere between chant and the blues. And there's prayer language, in our language. Some of the most moving poems have been spoken by the speaker as the sun comes up after we've danced all night. This is true all over the world, in nearly every culture. What winds up in books is a sliver of what we've been carrying since the beginning of time.

⋮

I can't help it. I love sweet sad ballads with heartache saxophone: Art Pepper, John Coltrane, especially Coltrane. The music breaks away at any crust of unlove to the longing for that home far from the density of years of soap opera on earth.

Remembering and imagination enter and leave from the same area of the soul.

There's a lullabye. Made to calm the ruler of sharp things.

When you grow up you either make uneasy peace with the density of destiny, and entertain the possibility of a reckless, cruel god, or watch television with the rest of the escapees.

We descend into a damp city. I anticipate the wet flowering of the desert. And it will remind me of the warm pools of moisture under your body after we have made love, when we are at the mercy of a tenderness beyond this world.

Some spirits go willingly (at death). In the tragedy of massacre the shock of rolling thoughtlessness can trap one in the house of disbelief. The body is a house of memory that decay cannot loosen.

And what of my friend who this afternoon weeded her garden, wielding a cigarette in one hand as she coughed with the cancer eating her, a friend on each side holding her up? She wants to leave with a little grace, yet doesn't want to leave at all. What do we know about anything?

We cannot escape memory, but carry it in us like a huge organ with lungs sucking air for survival. It is an organ like the skin, covering everything, but from the inside.

Was there ever mercy? Is Mercy an errant angel so horrified by cruel acts of humans she cannot bear to look on us? Mercy, come find us in the labyrinth of cruelty.

In Beethoven's house...there is no evidence of Beethoven's mother in this place. Who was she? There would be no Beethoven without her.

I felt the immensity of my anger for the first time. I felt totally present as yellow sharpened itself against the blue sky.

Each path reeked of afterbirth, rain and mice...Humans only think we can bend time into increments of money.

I think of names that have profoundly changed the direction of disaster. Of the raw whirling wind outlining femaleness emerging from the underworld.

SARAH MANGUSO

Q: I have read in one of your interviews that you ask your students to sit in silence for an hour, and then write about what happened without using "I". What is your intention with the exercise?

A: The goal is to force students to write, with deep engagement, about "nothing," and the lessons are twofold: that there's no such thing as nothing; and that there's always something to write about, even if it seems like nothing.

⋮

The trouble with comparing yourself to others is that there are too many others. Using all others as your control group, all your worst fears and all your fondest hopes are at once true. You are good; you are bad; you are abnormal; you are just like everyone else.

Inner beauty can fade too.

I used to avoid people when I was afraid I loved them too much. Ten years, in one case. Then, after I had been married long enough that I was married even in my dreams, I became able to go to those people, to feel that desire, and to know that it would stay a feeling.

Like a vase, a heart breaks once. After that, it just yields to its flaws.

We like stories that are false and seem true (realist novels), that are true and seem false (true crime), that are false and seem false (dragons and superheroes), or that are true and seem true, but it's harder to agree on what that is.

Just before the poetry reading starts, I ask the grown boy sitting next to me why he likes poetry, what happened to him, and he says, *I went to war*.

When the worst comes to pass, the first feeling is relief.

Rock faces, bodies of water, the crotch of a tree. It's harder to personify the sky.

Faced with a camera lens, hideously overwitnessed, I immediately start trying to impersonate myself.

After I stopped hoping to outgrow them, my fears were no longer a burden. Hope is what made them a burden.

Who seems a harmless fool to those above him is a malevolence to those beneath.

A nonspecific wish to change the world isn't about the world. It's about you.

Preferable to accepting one's insignificance is imagining the others hate you.

Nothing is more boring to me than the re-re-restatement that language isn't sufficiently nuanced to describe the world. Of course language isn't enough. Accepting that is the starting point of using it to capacity. Of increasing its capacity.

People like to tell my very successful friend that they, too, intend to write some books. He always answers, with big eyes and a ghoulish smile, *How hard could it be?*

It's impossible to fail if one doesn't know how the end should look. And it's impossible to succeed. But it's possible to enjoy.

Lack of effort poorly conceals lack of ability.

The trouble with setting goals is that you're constantly working toward what you used to want.

I want to shed my fears one by one until there is nothing left of me.

I look at young people and marvel at their ignorance of what's coming, and the old people look at me.

MAGGIE NELSON

Q: Among writers of short pieces in this collection, you seem most welcome to the presence of theoretical writing—feminist, psychological, literary or otherwise. Can you tell us how this enhances your observations and/or serves as a sounding board for your work?

A: I don't make hard distinctions between forms of writing, so I don't think of the 'real' or 'creative' work in one place and the 'theoretical' work in another. It's all one flow.

⋮

1. Suppose I were to begin by saying that I had fallen in love with a color. Suppose I were to speak this as though it were a confession; suppose I shredded my napkin as we spoke. *It began slowly. An appreciation, an affinity. Then, one day, it became more serious. Then* (looking into a teacup, its bottom stained with thin brown excrement coiled into the shape of a sea horse) *it became somehow personal.*

2. And so I fell in love with a color—in this case, the color blue—as if falling under a spell, a spell I fought to stay under and get out from under, in turns.

4. I admit that I may have been lonely. I know that loneliness can produce bolts of hot pain, a pain which, if it stays hot enough for long enough, can begin to simulate, or to provoke—take your pick—an apprehension of the divine. *(This ought to arouse our suspicions.)*

29. If a color cannot cure, can it at least incite hope? The blue collage you sent me so long ago from Africa, for example, made me hopeful. But not, to be honest, because of its blues.

35. Does the world look bluer from blue eyes? Probably not, but I choose to think so (self-aggrandizement).

38. For no one really knows what color is, where it is, even whether it is. *(Can it die? Does it have a heart?)* Think of a honeybee, for instance, flying into the folds of a poppy: it sees a gaping violet mouth, where we see an orange flower and assume that it's orange, that we're normal.

39. The Encyclopedia does not help. "If normally our perception of color involves 'false consciousness,' what is the right way to think of colors?" it

asks. "In the case of color, unlike other cases," it concludes, "false consciousness should be a case for celebration."

51. *You might as well act as if objects had the colors*, the Encyclopedia says.—Well, it is as you please. But what would it look like to act otherwise?

52. "We mainly suppose the experiential quality to be an intrinsic quality of the physical object"—this is the so-called systematic illusion of color. Perhaps it is also that of love. But I am not willing to go there—not just yet. I believed in you.

65. The instructions printed on the blue junk's wrapper: *Wrap Blue in cloth. Stir while squeezing the Blue in the last rinsing water. Dip articles separately for a short time; keep them moving.* I liked these instructions. I like blues that keep moving.

66. Yesterday I picked up a speck of blue I'd been eyeing for weeks on the ground outside my house, and found it to be a poison strip for termites. *Noli me tangere*, it said, as some blues do. I left it on the ground.

81. What I know: when I met you, a blue rush began. I want you to know, I no longer hold you responsible.

85. One afternoon in 2006, at a bookstore in Los Angeles, I pick up a book called *The Deepest Blue*. Having expected a chromatic treatise, I am embarrassed when I see the subtitle: *How Women Face and Overcome Depression.* I quickly return it to the shelf. Eight months later, I order the book online.

91. *Blue-eye,* archaic: "a blueness or dark circle around the eye, from weeping or other cause."

94.—Well then, it is as you please. This is the dysfunction talking. This is the disease talking. This is how much I miss you talking. This is the deepest blue, talking, talking, always talking to you.

95. But please don't write me again to tell me how you have woken up weeping. I already know how you are in love with your weeping.

96. For a prince of blue is a prince of blue because he keeps "a pet sorrow, a blue-devil familiar, that goes with him everywhere" (Lowell, 1870). This is how a prince of blue becomes a pain devil.

97. And now, I think, we can say: a glass bead may flush the world with color, but it alone makes no necklace. I wanted the necklace.

130. We cannot read the darkness. We cannot read it. It is a form of madness, albeit a common one, that we try.

131. "I just don't feel like you're trying hard *enough*," one friend says to me. How can I tell her that *not trying* has become the whole point, the whole plan?

133. I have been trying to place myself in a land of great sunshine, and abandon my will therewith.

136. "Drinking when you are depressed is like throwing kerosene on a fire," I read in another self-help book at the book store. *What depression ever felt like a fire?* I think, shoving the book back on the shelf.

220. Imagine someone saying, "Our fundamental situation is joyful." Now imagine *believing* it.

221. Or, forget belief: imagine *feeling*, even if for a moment, that it were true.

222. In January 2002, camping in the Dry Tortugas, on an island which is essentially an abandoned fort ninety miles north of Cuba, flipping through

a copy of *Nature* magazine. I read that the color of the universe (whatever this might mean—here I gather that it means the result of a survey of the spectrum of light emitted by around 200,000 galaxies) has finally been deduced. The color of the universe, the article says, is "pale turquoise." *Of course*, I think, looking out wistfully over the glittering Gulf. *I knew it all along. The heart of the world is blue.*

223. A few months later, back at home, I read somewhere else that this result was in error, due to a computer glitch. The *real* color of the universe, this article says, is light beige.

229. I am writing all this down in blue ink, so as to remember that all words, not just some, are written in water.

KARL JIRGENS

Q. Why have you engaged with extremely short forms of writing?

KJ: Historically, miniature art is highly valued. Micro-miniature art includes camel caravans walking through a needle's eye, a full backgammon board constructed on a single split rice-grain. Sometimes, less *is* more. Brevity may be the soul of wit, but life is mad, often absurd. We park on driveways, drive on parkways. We seek roots of meaning, wisdom's sources, fundamental notions, etymologies of etymologies, precis, sketches, snapshots. Brevity liberates readers' minds to contemplate larger ramifications. Acrostic. Haiku. Imagism. Limerick. Miniature forms abound. Aphorisms. Adages. Apophthegms. Bromides. Epigrams. Epithets. Glosses. Idioms. Bucket lists. Mantras. Maxims. Mottos. Quips. Witticisms. Clichés. Archetypes. Summaries. Boot Hill Epitaphs; "Here lies Lester Moore. Four slugs from a .44. No less, no more." How much can be said using the fewest words? Insight's bought, when simply wrought. Language taut, brings sage thought. Pure and simple facts are rarely pure, rarely simple, but simply put, open vistas. Life is short, uncertainty broad. Lucid words, do not cloud. Simple words for inspiration, may rouse thoughtful contemplation, sly quotations, cogitations, brief narrations, swift ovations. Only one thing you've got to know, language is as language does. Ain't no use to make a fuss, so long as your vernacular is acoustically spectacular.

⋮

"REALIZATION" (A CONCRETE REALITY)
A H
H A

CULTURAL EXCHANGE
WE / KNOW
OUI / NON

REMEMBERING A CHILDHOOD DREAM OF VISITING A FLORID ISLE
C R I B
R O S E
I S L E
B E E N

IT'S NOT ALL THAT
this
that

"That that is," with a Cockney accent
that that is, is. that that is not, is not. is that it? it is!

FRENCH MARINE CATASTROPHE
trois
cats
sank

THE TREACHERY OF WORDS
(Homage to Magritte)
THESE ARE NOT WORDS

DID YOU SEE A BUG?
G N A T
N O S E
A S K S
T E S T

GOBLIN TRAP
S L I P
L A M E
I M P S
P E S T

WAITING FOR FORTUNE'S AIM
S H O T
H O P E
O P E N
T E N D

MASS GRAVE
P L O T
L I M E
O M E N
T E N S

NASTY FROGGY GOES A-WOOING
F R O G
R A P E
O P E N
G E N T

DON PATERSON

Q: You write both poems and aphorisms. How does it happen that one work ends up as a poem, but another an aphorism? Do you decide beforehand?

A: Oh, there's no way I'd mistake one for the other. To be honest, I only write aphorisms when I can't write anything else, and therefore not only reluctantly, but often in a foul mood—a flavour I fear they retain. For me, an aphorism is just a record of a sudden (and often momentary) conviction. By contrast, a poem is a way of me working out what I think when I don't actually know. If I get a 'good idea for a poem' I run a mile, because I now understand that's not how poems come into being; but I do think that you get an idea for an aphorism. Maybe that's all an aphorism *is*: an idea for an aphorism. The falling short, the self-defeatedness, is weirdly built into the form. My poem will fail too, but it always sets forth with a wee heart full of misplaced hope and a silly little spring in its step. And unlike the poem, I don't think aphorism is a culturally important form; I may have angered other aphorists by saying so, but I have royalty statements that seem to back this up.

Q: There seems to be a nondualist bent to some of your work that seems to be inspired by Asian philosophies. Do you care to tell us about this influence?

A: Nihilism has a bad rap in the west, whereas Eastern philosophy can detect and distinguish between all sorts of nothing; it also understands the difference between skepticism and cynicism, while we *claim* to, but actually still struggle. This has a grim corollary, which is that we suspend our skepticism whenever we think we're fighting our cynicism. (This is why so many liberals are far too keen to credit Trump with a 'presidential' act, when they should just see a stopped clock.) I tend to think the aphorism peaked with Cioran, and I hear Nagarjuna in him all the time; I probably try to steer my philosophical course between the two, insofar as I'm conscious of one. Some translate *svabhava*– 'emptiness,' sort of—as 'substance,' which is pretty damn funny, if that's our best shot. I'm a neutral monist, which is partly a lousy attempt to accommodate nondualism within a Western framework. I think a) there's only matter, but b) that matter is very weird. More generally, there are a lot of false choices presented to us (and I certainly think you don't have to choose between serious and funny). So if you hear a 'nondualist bent,' that's pleasing. Dualism is just another cultural lie, I think, another dud metaphor—like the future being ahead of us, death being an enemy, heaven being up, and life being a journey. These things will literally kill us all. If the aphorism has any purpose at all, it's to prick a hole in them and start letting the air out.

⋮

In all art, the function of the ego is to drive you to the gig, then keep the van ticking over while you perform without it. Those who fail to do so are easy to identify: they all *shake*.

Amazing that the chess clock never found a more general application. A more enlightened society would have made it as indispensable to conversation as shoes to walking.

Strange ceremonies no one told you you would have to observe. The first lover to die on you. You've made love to a dead woman; the white limbs that were folded round you only last year are already rotting into the earth. You *must* have missed something the last time, some sign, some undertone of *départ* to the proceedings.

The trees in winter, those exact diagrams of all our dead yearnings.

Time heals so well it erases us; we *are* its wounds.

No email for an hour. The *bastards*.

My admiration for him was too high, and destroyed any chance we might have had of friendship. Every email to him I drafted and redrafted into idiocy, solecism, and quixotic affectation. I began to resent him, to devise ways I might discredit him, *depose* him...and then understand why he had been wary of me from the start.

Like every other literary critic, Bloom credits the writer with far too much interest in literature. Such as it exists, the Anxiety of Influence is mostly a business between contemporaries. The tensions are all sibling, not Oedipal.

Such is E's need to be loved, he experiences the casual indifference of a stranger and a snub from his closest friend as the *same torment*.

The sadness of old shoes. Putting them on again, I suddenly remember all the old friends I haven't seen for ages; and then *why*.

A correction made to work more than five years old is less a revision than the cancellation of another man's opinion.

A style is a strategy of evasion.

My absolute blind fury at J's obituaries, as he denied me the profound pleasure of being jealous of him any longer…though even in death, I could still discern the cast of ambition in his face. No doubt he's already making his way up the infernal ladder, and has risen to some subaltern of the demonic.

Hell is an enforced solitude, heaven a voluntary one.

Our most grievous error is to think our incarnation some kind of cosmic privilege. We fall into time as a dead leaf into a river.

She was not comfortable with the idea of him alone in her house, less for those secrets of hers he might discover than for the lack of them: the lack was, in fact, her worst secret.

All our instruments are accurate, except the clock. The clock holds up two sticks in the air and draws a conclusion.

The *emphasis* is all wrong; the tale of his life will read like a great book underlined by an idiot.

I love the way we all suddenly stop traducing our enemy when we hear they have a cancer or have suffered a stroke. If only we could always keep in the front of our minds that we are *all* dying.

The true avant-garde cultivate the territories others merely stake out. They are, furthermore, the real subversives among us, since they never draw attention to themselves through the crime of originality.

The first procedure of good style is the inversion of the form in which the idea occurred to the thinker.

We could easily have evolved eyelids thick enough to keep out the light, but we still need to see the shadows fall across it. We're not yet *safe*.

I considered myself immune to the sirens of suicide, until one morning I somehow managed to alert myself to a grievous sea change; the idea had just crossed my mind *casually*. Since that moment I have been roped to the mast of myself.

Desire is the inconvenience of its object. Lourdes isn't Lourdes if you live in Lourdes.

A poem is a little machine for remembering itself.

With your back to the wall, always pay a compliment. Even your mugger or torturer is not immune to flattery, and still capable of being a little disarmed by a word of congratulation on their choice of footwear or superior technique.

Whale to the ocean, bird to the sky, man to his dream.

No sense steps into the same word twice.

I had never had such a thing before: a *declared* enemy. But I'd be lost without him now. It's a feeling so close to love. I *made* him, as one makes a poem or a child, by accident and design.

Wouldn't it be wonderful to start our children's spiritual education at the age of six with the honest opener: *Children—I'm afraid no one has the first clue why we're here.*

Your manifest uncertainty is the best guarantor of the truth of your statement, not your wise voice.

"Now I'll read a long poem." And as one heart, our hearts sunk; somewhere I heard a hundred slide trombones slump weakly. It was then I finally admitted to myself that a poetry reading was *no night out.*

In the end, the desolate age always turns instinctively to classicism, which if nothing else legislates against certain kinds of disappointment.

The rose's night-black is as true as her day-red.

As we think of the dead, so the immortals think of us: as a fraternity of ghosts, the *ones-who-pass-through* . . .

Beware the obsessive between obsessions: if his brain doesn't eat itself, it will eat yours.

The worst thing about thinking nothing of yourself is that you assume that your behavior has no consequence. This makes you much more dangerous than the egomaniac, who at least spends all his time calculating for his own effect.

You are wrong about T's innocence being evidence of his "good heart"; the fact that a washing machine or toaster has no unconscious motive doesn't make it a saint.

Poets dream within their imaginative elsewheres. In Scotland we live with very occasional illumination, so ours is actually a rather sunlit verse; by contrast, the Spanish poet is stalked by shadow.

Always plant a quiet line that critics can damn you with; this proves they were always hunting for it.

Those wholly estranged from themselves only have two real homes: the monastery or the stage.

CHARLES BERNSTEIN

Q: Too abstract, don't you think, too much in the head?

A: I don't know much about affect but I know what I don't like.

Q: But even doubt has its limits, no?

A: Those ardent in their beliefs and certain of God's will are the faithless ones. Feeling superior to the self-righteous makes you that. (Taking pleasure in piety is piteous.)

Q: Can there be a perfect aphorism?

A: There is no perfect in poetry; but there can be more perfection.

Q: Could you expand on that?

A: The slow apple catches the worm. In other words, the early bird catches dawn but sleeps through dusk.

. . .

AMBERIANUM

[Philosophical Fragments of Caudio Amberian]

Abolens sensus numquam liberare cogitatione.
Abolishing reason will never free thought.

Etiam homo fastus scribere posse bonum carmen. Sed suus non amo.
Even a self-righteous man can write a good poem. But it's not likely.

Praecaveo osor qui clamat "odisti!"
Beware the bigot who shouts out "bigot!"

Nonnumquam homo qui mendacii loquimini veritatem.
Even a liar sometimes must tell the truth.

O dii magna! Protecut nobis adversum malis qui consumuntur per justitia.
May the gods save us from those consumed by their righteousness.

Colaphus est chiridotus punctum.
A cuff is not a sleeve.

Aestas alga mutates in hiberna malogranatum
Summer seaweed becomes winter pomegranates.

Si paratextus fortior poema sequitur fornicando fortior amor?
If paratext is more important than poem, does it follow that love is more important than sex?

Perceptio est scriptum.
Perception is textual.

Omni scriptura est pupilla.
All texts are orphans.

Perspicientia est sensus vigalantis.
Knowledge is a matter of minding sense.

Ubi erraverit caper detondetur vitulum.
Where the goat strays the calf is shorn.

Rarus est maeror nomas.
Seldom is grief misplaced.

Omne iter fluxum.
Every journey takes a turn.

Cultura est opinabilis.
Cultivation is a manner of opinion.

In fragmenta veritas.
Truth is in pieces.

Vivis et vigeo. Argumentum injustitia deos.
The fact that you are alive and thriving is proof that the gods are not just.

Remissio prope nihil. Desiderium dono divum.
Forgiveness is overrated. Regret is a gift of gods.

Quid nunc videtur priori numquam imaginabilis.
What was unimaginable an hour ago is unforgettable now.

Proximi sui ruina unius hominis felicitatem.
One man's catastrophe is his neighbor's good fortune.

Servus absolvo illusion licentia. Dominus amat fraudis.
A slave is free of the illusion of freedom from which his master takes pleasure.

Virtus est selectivam.
Virtue is selective.

Coitus est bonitas plus quam amor. Est tangibili.
Sex is more virtuous than love because it is more tangible.

Amor abducit lubido.
Love turns many from desire.

In vino exiguum clinamen veritas.
In wine truth swerves.

Sensus mentis dolum.
Perception is the finest trick of the mind.

Veritas nondum visibilis.
The truth remains to be seen.

Salus in numeris donec numerus vester ascendit.
There is safety in numbers until your number is up.

Numquam nominare inane vacuum.
Never call a void a void.

Sine pullos nihilum ova.
If there were no chickens there'd be no eggs.

Ignorantiam didicit.
Ignorance is learned.

Odium contagiosa est.
Hatred is contagious.

Maximo sinceritatis ironia.
Irony is the perfection of sincerity.

Veritas est scortum sumptuosus
Truth is a pricey whore.

Judaeorum dabo optimus pretium.
Jews will give you the best price.

Si videris Judaeus, dicere salve pro me.
If you see a Jew be sure to say I said hello.

Omni infringes punctum impotens etiam amare.
Everything breaks at its weakest point including love.

Fragilitas solicito amatio.
Fragility is the root of love.

Quasi pardus est Judaeus. Sed absque maculis.
A Jew is like a leopard without the spots.

⋮

Caudio Amberian was a Jewish poet and sophist of the first century C.E. (circa 30-75). He was likely born near Alexandria and spoke or read Aramaic, Hebrew, and Greek. He may have studied with Philo before moving to Rome around 60. In Rome, Amberian started a small school for sophistry, where he engaged students in Socratic-style dialogs. In addition, Amberian was a counselor to Nero in the last years of his reign, following the fire, and he helped set the ground for the move of Josephus and his entourage from Jerusalem to Rome in 71. The only previous translation of Amberian's work, an untitled poem, was published in *Girly Man*.

At his school in Rome, Amberian spoke in a broken or pidgin Latin that some of his students called "barbaric." The only record we have of his writing are the Latin transcriptions made by these notoriously unreliable and sometimes hostile students. The *Amberianum* was reconstructed from shreds and shards at the Sid Caesar Center for Dysraphic Studies. Missing words and the seaming of disconnected parts likely mar the work. The Latin manuscript was discovered on October 4, 1895, buried under a former Minsk dry goods store. The story of the miraculous finding of the *Amberianum* has been told in the award-winning book, *The Oy!: How the World Became Pataquerical.*

SHARON DOLIN

Q: You work in aphoristic sequences. Each aphorism either builds on the previous ones, or they all work together, creating something like montage or collage. Can you describe how these aphoristic sequences work differently than, say, adjacent lines in a poem?

A: Each aphorism is a whole fragment, to paraphrase Yahia Lababidi, while each aphoristic sequence is a fragmentary whole composed of these whole fragments. Its spirit is akin to poetry because the sequence is non-linear, associative, peripatetic; in this sense, the aphoristic sequence is closest in form to the essay. Each time I write a new sequence, I am assaying this form, trying out what becomes of the interplay between self and place. Each aphorism accrues, perambulates, and elaborates on the evolving themes. I would say there is much more white space between each aphorism than there is between adjacent lines of poetry.

The lines of a poem, on the other hand, are more closely knit; they have a musicality to them that aphorisms lack. Some of my aphorisms could stand alone; in this sense they are whole fragments. My poetic lines rely on the visual as well as the auditory music of the entire poem. Through enjambment, the poetic line is always dynamic, interacting with preceding and succeeding lines so that to isolate one line creates a hole in the net of meaning while the isolated aphorism within a sequence is linked by the holes. In other words, aphorisms in a sequence emphasize the holes in the net; poems emphasize the net. Each aphorism is a small island, each sequence an archipelago.

⋮

from THE BOOK OF LOST APHORISMS

The first aphorism was lost. All others are in search of that first aphorism. Thus, there is always something abandoned, belated, or mournful in the aphorism. Some failure or irrecoverable loss.

The more the blank book of aphorisms fills up, the more each one empties itself out.

The goal of becoming lost is to be lost to all one's worries, all one's woes— all those weights holding you down, as in a hot-air balloon, that keep you from soaring.

Why do we gaze at ruins like Ephesus? To fill in what has crumbled or to be reminded of what all human efforts amount to?

To travel is to absent oneself for a greater presence outside the self. Look! A stop sign you finally attend to: *DUR!*

Nostalgia for the lost aphorism—its ability to compress truth into a pistachio nut.

In a country where many do not drink, what a relief to dwell on his lost and future kisses, headier than raki.

The embrace of betraying lovers is like the handshake between thieves: At some point they will betray/steal from each other. They know no other nature.

Concision is the first and only rule of the aphorism. Only the lost aphorism came close.

To click one's bill like the African storks nesting on top of the broken pediment.

The wisdom of Artemis: to know when it is time to migrate from Ephesus to Africa.

After dwelling for so long in the absence of kindness, honesty, decency, no wonder you prize these qualities—like exotic arabesques—above all others.

Lost? Found only on the Sabbath in between the candle flames.

In dreams, one glimpses the ladder to the lost aphorism.

Or the lost lover.

The absent husband (and his cruel neglect) are not buried in the lost aphorism. Because of your anger, he lies unburied inside you and you must figure out how to expel and fling him into the desert of lost chances.

Catalan poet Gemma Gorga's *Book of Minutes* is a diminutive, metaphysical book of hours consisting of sixty prose poems. They display a disarming simplicity, at times offering meditations on the soul and on language itself. Gorga uses the prose poem as the site of exploration—of the self and the cosmos, of time and relationships. The more one meditates on these poems, the more they unfold in the mind's eye, like paper flowers blossoming in water.

—Sharon Dolin

[Every night, when I turn off the light]

Every night, when I turn off the light, the heavy glass of consciousness is spilled and the world ends with me. In the dark, I pray God hurries to invent a circular book, a book that links the end to the beginning, a book that promises a new genesis after each apocalypse.

[At night, questions are phosphorescent]

At night, questions are phosphorescent and are watching us with their cat's eyes. Phosphorescent as buried bones. And like bones, hard, strange, and persisting beyond answers.

[I raise the blinds]

I raise the blinds so light may enter. I part the curtains so light may enter. I close my eyes so light may enter.

I throw a pebble into water]

I throw a pebble into water, and the water learns the word *shipwreck*. I pass my hand over paper, and the paper learns the word *caress*. I enter the sea and the waves learn how to say my name.

[Happiness resembles a monosyllable]

Happiness resembles a monosyllable. Due to its structural simplicity. Also, due to the brevity with which it visits our mouth.

ALEX STEIN

Q: What guidance would you offer an aspiring artist?

A: The longing to create makes the artist fecund. The longing to be of service makes the artist profound. The longing to create profundity makes the artist sterile.

Q: Anything else?

Damage makes artists and loss provokes inspiration. Art is a poultice mixed to heal a wound.

Q: At one time, you described yourself as a "Zen poet". How do you define "Zen"?

Zen is an order, that's all. Neither better nor worse, fundamentally, than any other order. It is not a mystic order. If anything, it is a utilitarian order that occasionally opens out into the mystic the way a hoe in a field occasionally upturns a truffle. I can also tell you what I was told, when I asked the same question: *Zen is a wound.*

:

First came creation, unconscious, primeval,
and inside creation was everything,
even the seed of its own realization,
awaiting rebirth.

In fields of blueberries, the faces of my wives and daughters. In the star-apple tree, the children of my children's children.

The artist is on a swing; one that carries him back and forth between knowing and unknowing, and asks that he make a home in both places. But how can one make a home of unknowing?

On the bank of an ancient pond,
the frog, knowing only this life,
awaits the rising moon.

The truth, the truth is on fire.
Time-present is an all-consuming pyre.
Time-future, the shadow of desire.
Time-past, a desperate liar.
The truth, the truth is on fire.

What does it mean if I have a belief? That I must nurture and cultivate that belief? Tend and encourage it, until it grows from a tiny seedling into a mighty tree with limbs that block out the sky?

"I is another," wrote Rimbaud, of his poetic self.
And Nietzsche, in conversation with Lou-Andreas Salome, referred to himself as a "tertium quid," meaning "a disembodied third person or entity."
"It composes," Nietzsche told Salome, "I am neither mind nor body."
For the poet, inspiration is the "third entity." For the lover, dissolution.

We each have a pattern of behavior into which we fall, when the construct of the self that we most vaunt, the idea of self to which we have longest adhered, is in danger of dissolution. It is probably a fear of death reflex, something like the start one experiences, on occasion, falling into sleep.

Many more things belong in the category of common sense than we sometimes allow for. It makes common sense to be candid. If only because candor brings clarity. And without clarity, we are in bondage.

The history of art is like a stratified fossil record of evolving human consciousness. It tells of our submariner existence in the sea of unknowing.

If you could declare a moratorium on anything, what would you choose?
Unkind thoughts.

The whole of chess is contained within a single chessman.

Star-dwellers, spirits,
they too, have families/histories,
they too, suffer confusions,
and bear mysteries.

Each poem is a little birth and every poet is a mid-wife.

The promises of poetry are: "full return on your investment" and "you will never be lonely." The promises of poetry are: "insight brings us to understanding" and "there is something that can be grasped and held."

   The promises of poetry are: many-petaled and frequently redacted.

The blossoms from a plum tree,
being carried away on spring winds,
obliquely evoke our fall from Grace.

"Artistry!" is the echo that returns
when you shout 'Art History!' down a canyon.

DINTY W. MOORE

Q: Can you tell us how your meditative practice has affected your writing practice, and vice versa?

A: I'm not sure my meditative practice has done much to influence the author side of me, since the striving necessary to be a published writer is clearly contradictory to the non-attachment tenets of Buddhism. I do know, however, that certain lessons I've learned over the years as an artist—trust your instinct, don't grasp too tightly, be open to surprise—made me a natural Buddhist, even before I studied enough to understand the connections.

.
.
.

NUMBER NINE

I believe in everything until it's disproved.
So I believe in fairies, the myths, dragons.
It all exists, even if it's in your mind.
JOHN LENNON

The Beatles appeared on The Ed Sullivan Show on February 9, 1964, and I succumbed like everyone else. Cuban missiles and Cold War had defined our lives for far too long. America needed a diversion.

Enter Ringo.

–9–

In my bedroom on 9th Street, my transistor radio under the pillow, I anticipated each new single:

"Can't Buy Me Love," "Eight Days a Week," "Do You Want to Know a Secret?"

Boy, did I ever.

–9–

For instance, where was Paul?

In 1968, soon after Martin Luther King and Bobby Kennedy were gunned down by 'lone assassins,' a Detroit disk jockey received a phone call advising him to listen closely to the endings of certain Beatles songs and to play other tracks in reverse.

He did just that, and discovered John muttering "I buried Paul" at the conclusion of "Strawberry Fields Forever." In addition, the line "Paul is dead man, miss him, miss him" could be heard—if you wanted badly enough to hear it—in the space connecting "I'm So Tired" to "Blackbird."

–9–

On "Revolution 9," the disconcerting eight-minute sound collage on the second disk of *The Beatles* (aka *The White Album*), a male voice repeats the words "number nine, number nine, number nine." Played in reverse, the brief snippet sounds eerily like someone straining to say "turn me on dead man."

The song scared the crap out of me, in either direction. John and Paul had been trotting out a lot of peculiar ideas in that period, but the bizarre cacophony of nightmarish noise on "Revolution 9" went beyond anything I could explain or had ever expected.

—9—

Truth be told, I was less frightened by the notion that The Beatles had put the reverse message onto the album intentionally than by the more startling idea that this dark message may have ended up on the disk some other way—that the words "turn me on dead man" were *not* intentional.

First Jack, then Martin, then Bobby.

It was not too much to imagine—not for me at least—that imperceptible evil was moving, somewhere, underneath the visible surface of the world.

Or in the grooves.

Evil itself pressed into a black vinyl disk.

—9—

John always had a thing about the number nine.

He was born on October 9th.

His son Sean was born on October 9th.

Brian Epstein, The Beatles' manager, first saw the group on November 9th.

John met Yoko on yet another November 9th.

For a while in his youth, John lived at 9 Newcastle Road.

Liverpool has nine letters.

—9—

"Nine seems to be my number so I've stuck with it," John once explained, "and it's the highest number in the universe; after that you go back to one."

—9—

The Beatles drifted back to one—back, that is, to solo careers—soon after the "Paul is dead" debacle petered out. By 1971, John had moved to New York, and within weeks of his arrival, he was meeting with Jerry Rubin and other members of the New Left, planning an anti-war Woodstock.

The following February, a secret memo was sent to Richard Nixon by Senator Strom Thurmond pointing out the danger Lennon's activism might cause to Nixon's re-election, and suggesting a termination of Lennon's visa.

But Thurmond was late to the party. J. Edgar Hoover's FBI had been watching Lennon for years.

—9—

In February 1974, Samuel J. Byck, distraught that Nixon had ignored struggling small businessmen, tried to hijack a commercial airliner and coerce the crew to crash into The White House. Byck went to the Baltimore airport, forced his way onto a flight by fatally shooting an airport policeman, and ordered the crew to depart. After the crew informed him that they could not go anywhere without removing the wheel blocks, Byck shot them.

He then realized there was no one to fly the plane. So he shot himself.

This was 27 years before 9-11.

The plane was a DC9.

—9—

At various points in history, the number nine has been considered ominous. In the year 999, many Europeans gave away property and forgave debts, believing the world was on the verge of a Second Coming.

—9—

Nine is also mathematically unique.

Multiply any number by 9, and the sum of the digits will come to 9 (e.g., 5 x 9 = 45; 4 + 5 = 9).

Reverse the digits, and the number you get (54) will be a multiple of 9.

–9–

My favorite line from the song "Revolution 9," by the way, was not the one spoken by the sound engineer but one spoken by Yoko, John's muse:

"If you become naked," she whispered, never completing the thought.

I was in ninth grade.

It seemed like an invitation.

–9–

The same year that Nixon was forced to resign his office—on August 9th—John Lennon released his ninth solo album, in the ninth month. On it was the song "#9 Dream," which some say predicted John's own assassination.

–9–

Mark David Chapman, Lennon's murderer, heard voices. "I used to fantasize that I was a king, and I had all these Little People around me and that they lived in the walls," he would explain later. "And that I was their hero and…and I was on TV every day…and that I was important."

Chapman came to believe that certain albums held secret messages. Chapman was a particular fan of Todd Rundgren, and presumed that the title of Rundgren's 1980 album—*Deface the Music*—was a distinct signal.

–9–

So, on December 8, 1980, Chapman waited outside the Dakota apartment building for John and Yoko to return from a recording session. When Lennon exited his limousine, Chapman called out his name—"Mr. Lennon"—then fired four pistol shots, killing the former Beatle.

–9–

Across from the Dakota later that evening, thousands of mourners began to congregate. Among them was John Hinckley.

Hinckley had seen the movie *Taxi Driver* fifteen times and had developed an obsession with Jodie Foster, the childish prostitute in the film, and began to stalk her, fantasizing about various ways to capture her attention, including possibly hijacking an airplane.

Instead, Hinckley settled on assassination as his best strategy to win Foster's heart, and on March 30, 1981, fired six times at President Ronald Reagan outside of the Hilton Hotel in Washington, DC.

In Hinckley's hotel room, police found a John Lennon calendar and paperback copy of *The Catcher in the Rye*.

–9–

Had Reagan died, he would have continued an odd numerical string.

Starting in the mid-1800s, every president who was elected in a year ending in a zero has died in office. William Harrison (elected in 1840) died of pneumonia. Abraham Lincoln (1860) was assassinated, as were James Garfield (1880) and William McKinley (1900). Warren Harding (1920) died of a heart attack, and Franklin Roosevelt (1940) of cerebral hemorrhage.

John F. Kennedy, of course, was elected in 1960.

–9–

George W. Bush became President in 2000, but did not die in office.

Perhaps this is because Ronald Reagan broke the curse.

Or perhaps, as some believe, because he was not *actually* elected.

–9–11–

On the 11th day of the ninth month of the year 2001, two terrorist-controlled planes destroyed the twin towers.

The towers, side by side, looked like the number 11.

The first plane to hit the towers was American Airlines Flight 11.

After September 11th there are 111 days left to the end of the year.

New York City has 11 letters.

So does the name George W. Bush.

—11-

So it is either nine or eleven we should fear most.

Or the Bush family.

Or Beatles records, played backwards.

—11-

Or it could be me.

My name has 11 letters, and I was born on August 11th.

I once saw George W. Bush, waving in my direction from the back of a presidential limousine.

There was a prominent rose bush in my family's backyard.

On 9th Street.

The rose bush was covered with beetles.

The walrus was Paul.

Goo goo ga joob.

—11-

Mathematicians will tell you that even this many concurrences can be pure coincidence. "We're awash in a torrent of names, numbers, dates, addresses, acronyms, telephone calls, e-mails, calendars, birth dates," Temple University professor John Paulos (nine letters) has explained. "In reality, the most astonishingly incredible coincidence imaginable would be the complete absence of all coincidences."

—9-

Statistician Persi Diaconis (thirteen letters) studies coincidence and believes we are "hard-wired" to overreact to patterns and repetition. In fact, being a bit paranoid can be an advantage for survival.

"It goes back to primitive man," Diaconis explains. "You look in the bush, it looks like stripes, you'd better get out of there before you determine the odds that you're looking at a tiger. The cost of being flattened by the tiger is high."

The cost of fleeing is low.

–9-

And of course, conspiracy theories can be oddly reassuring.

Given two options—that the words "turn me on dead man" appeared on "Revolution 9" because

John Lennon put them there, or

for reasons none of us can comprehend,

there is good reason the latter scared me far worse than the former. No one wants to think that bad things derive from purely unseen forces, that some cloak of evil exists well beyond our perception. Such a belief would be too frightening.

–9-

In fact, if the entire canon of horrible global events—assassinations, climate change, levee breaches, terrorism, starvation—could be laid at the door of nefarious cartels with far more power than we can even imagine (e.g., Halliburton), then we as individuals would be off the hook. How nice, to be off the hook, excused any moral or political responsibility for the crisis at hand.

And being off the hook has an additional benefit: we are freed from having to participate in any painful remedy. We can over-consume like hogs. Cheat on our taxes. Drive our SUVs.

-9-

The Federal Bureau of Investigation (twenty-eight letters) was finally forced to release John Lennon's files, seventeen years after his death.

One portion of the top-secret dossier began with the lyrics to the song "John Sinclair," lyrics which had been 'classified' despite the fact that they were available in any record store, on John's album cover. Another portion of the FBI file detailed incendiary slogans regularly squawked by a parrot belonging to one of John's anti-war friends. A third section contained the FBI's appraisal of the musical talent of Lennon's wife.

Yoko, a field agent dutifully reported, "can't even remain on key."

-11-

I, for one, am entirely grateful that the government kept on top of Yoko's vocal ability, because she, after all, was the one who broke up The Beatles. And her family played a key behind-the-scenes role in bankrolling the attack on Pearl Harbor.

-9-

You didn't know that?

Yoko was born into one of Japan's most powerful lineages. She attended school with Emperor Hirohito's sons, Akihito and Yoshi. Her paternal great-grandfather, Atsushi Saisho, descends from a 9th Century emperor, and her maternal grandfather, the billionaire Zenjiro Yasuda, headed up one of Japan's richest business cartels, both before and after the War.

Rearrange the letters of Atsushi Saisho, by the way, and you get "Ah So, USA is Shit."

-9-

Could it be *any* more obvious?

H. L. HIX

FALSE POSITIVES

Q: Some people say their writing is their "religion". How would you characterize your relationship to your writing?

A: I'm trying to withhold consent from what Lauren Berlant calls the "meta-structure of consent."

Q: Could you expand a little on that, in a layperson's terms?

A: Berlant observes that our life situations (such as our political institutions) often are arranged so that decisions by, and agreements between, individuals take place within a field tightly constrained by prior, "larger," unquestioned terms, typically "givens" that the parties don't even notice, so that even what is intended as dissent can actually further strengthen what creates that from which the dissenter intends to dissent. I'm trying through my writing to learn to be aware of those larger constraints that are (now Wittgenstein) "like a pair of glasses on our nose through which we see whatever we look at."

⋮

Meaning means form. Form forms meaning.

To secure beauty and truth, practice insecurity.

No self sees itself except by seeing itself as other-than-self.

One metaphor to tend the hearth; one, the fields.

She sang against the last violence, to denounce the next.

Recognize the *magnitude* of otherness in its *multiplicity*.

Awakened from dream into dreamt.

Process, as claimed, but still product, condemned to commodification.

Only what belongs to no one belongs to all.

I thought I knew. I should have known better.

Until we name past trauma, we are powerless to prevent future trauma. Still, we ought not mistake the naming for the prevention.

Trapped in this my body, I am equally astonished that nothing else is, and that I myself am.

We may, and should, reason toward conscience. And *imagine* toward conscience.

An ocean separates art from life, but still their shorelines match.

Of continental drift all I can feel is the occasional quaking.

Like a language, a culture lives by, or dies for lack of, translation.

No thinking without dualisms, but we can think *with* dualisms *away from* dualisms rather than toward them.

Rebut one silence with another.

Surrounded by shouting, share a whisper.

To speak out I might take up my pen, or I might set it down.

What we see matters less than what we see by.

God didn't value the Tower of Babel, but nothing compels us to concur in that judgment.

Before it became a tool of corporate data collection, intertextuality was an instrument of song.

They also swerve who don't command much freight.

Had it tributaries, this inland sea might host more life.

No ideal more absurd and impossible than "self-definition."

To invent a vocabulary adequate to the unspeakable.

To hear not the speaker but the spoken to.

Brick laments as ruin what weeds relish as restoration.

No one owns the language, but anyone willing to homestead in it can find a place.

Divinize humanity, to humanize.

Sense like a beast, think like a god.

The inner world and the outer. Only what inhabits neither can see both.

I am not yet music, but I have not stopped trying to be.

Testify to one wrong, resist another.

What to do with my degree from the college of inconsequence?

To make the present most intensely present, should I look toward the future or the past?

The one who critiques Our Way is not one of Us.

If it echoes around the canyon, is it still one cry from one bird?

As in horse training, addressing something directly may not be the most intimate approach.

Extension of who I listen to enlarges what I hear.

Language does enough excluding, without our inviting national alliances to do more.

Let us now praise porous borders.

The nothing that is not aware, and the nothing that is.

The faults in speech speak, too, not only the perfections.

So immersed are we in instrumentality that making nothing happen is the only form opposition can take.

I cling to what is slipping away, not so that it will *not* slip away, but so that I *will*.

MICHAEL MARTONE

Q: You've spoken and written about new forms of writing out-pacing the genres covered in academia. Unsigned anonymous digital blogs, collaborative writing, etc. Where does—or doesn't—extremely short writing fit into this picture?

A: I wouldn't use the notion of "outpacing." That implies that the academy (that great ancient sorting machine) is in the business of happily inventing new categories of study to add to the ones that already exist. That is to say the academy works hard to make these new forms of writing "fit" into courses of study. I see it as slightly more confrontational. The fit of new forms of writing is not to fit. The business of boundary work by artists is to convulse and disrupt the critical patrolling of borders, the policing of critical categories, and the determinations of quality. You know, a poem not meaning but being. The critic, the academic is the one who decides, makes judgments, orders, creates hierarchies. I believe it is not the job of the artist to write to those fixed positions but invent new forms and ways of writing at will, not caring what it means or where it goes or if it is good. The risk is to become invisible, idiosyncratic, as humans seem to need categories in order to see to see. But the job is to defamiliarize, to not fit in by design.

⋮

POSTCARDS

THE MORNING AFTER THE BLUE MOON

There in the black paving the shallow scoop of the pothole, bruised debris and dust, haloed by the sketchy orbits of spray paint. Don't miss missing this.

THAT OLD LACTOSE MOON

No one thinks anymore that the moon is made of cheese, green cheese to boot. Green as in new, young, a cream cheese. So that old wheel up there now, the blue one, Love, is ripe and waxing riper. Look, the deep blue vein of aging, vivid geology of rot.

DON'T LOOK NOW

But behind your back the Blue Moon inches up your spine while the nameless sun sets, setting the sea to boil.

You are an island surrounded by horizon, your sight line a zippered equator. Look! Look now!

UNDER CONSTRUCTION

The moon must get its parts somewhere. Why not here, an island in the middle of nowhere. A quarry of the building blocks of planets and hill enough to take the edge off. The light. The light seems to have its own light. It reflects on its own reflection. A wave. A particle of its own partaking.

EAR OF CORN

Not so much a pop or even a knuckle crack the shock shocking as it telescopes joint to joint in the stalk.

You can get lost out there in all that corn, lured by the silky siren, the wind winding through the silk, shucking off the sense of the deep shadow. The shush.

IN THE BLUE KITCHEN

There is you, setting the blue flame beneath the blue kettle.

There is me, seeing through the sweating glass the sliver of blue in the soul of the ice cube.

IN THE CENTRAL MIDDLE SCHOOL

In the middle of nowhere, on the edge of the central, nothing is abstract, all concrete, aggregate & cement. Even the clouds are brutal, chiseled from that sad façade, the rain.

NORTH OF NORTH

That first night after the first night I met her, while she slept, I searched around in her things.

There in her underwear drawer was a little sachet sweating the scent of some pine tree up north. I knew, sap that I am, home.

FIRST TIME

"What are those strange clouds?" I asked, pointing east over the Sound.

"They're not clouds," he said, "they're mountains."

"O!" I said and "O!" again and again, all the way down the range, a cascade, all the way to Rainier it was raining mountains.

ON A HOT SUMMER'S DAY, THE NATIONAL ZOO'S LARGE CAT CURATOR SELECTS, FROM THE RESTAURANT-GRADE FREEZER, A FROZEN BLOOD BLOCK LICK FOR THE SWELTERING TIGERS

There's no mistaking the color. These puck licks we call bloodsicles. My warm-blooded fingers melt into the cube on the way to the air-conditioned cage.

"QUEEN OF THE DEAD," A CITIZEN SCIENTIST VOLUNTEER OF THE UNITED STATES GEOLOGICAL SURVEY'S NATIONAL MAP CORPS, EDITS A TOPO MAP POINT IN HARLAN COUNTY

This cemetery, a structure feature (as are schools, prisons, POs . . .) demands revision. My contoured focus: Tend the dead. My declivity, my orientation.

ANA MARIA SHUA

TRANSLATED BY RHONDA DAHL BUCHANAN

Q: Can you describe the alchemy that occurs when you fuse traditional stories—myths and fairy tales—with your contemporary sensibility?

If I could describe the alchemy, then it wouldn't be alchemy but science. And it's 100% alchemy of course. All I can say is I love myths and fairy tales. They are alive and always contemporary, and have crossed the barriers of time and space to come to us, to touch our souls and minds. For these reasons, I have a deep respect for them and I try to show that when I work with them.

Q: Do these fusions ever surprise even you?

Everything I write surprises me. Even this simple answer. After so many years of writing, I have learned that you might think everything is clear in your mind, but then it changes when you try to put it into written words. I love reading folk tales, myths, and legends, and never know what is going to strike me or provoke my need to write about it. Although these are ancient tales, I find in them something that is still relevant to mankind now and probably forever more.

⋮

What would you have liked to have been if you weren't what you are? the journalist asks the vampiress. I would have loved to have partaken of the blood of a journalist, she replies, much more interested in his jugular than his microphone.

My daughter uses the same word for feet, birds, and belly buttons. This is a foot, baby, not a bird, I correct her adamantly, while holding in my hands one of her warm, throbbing little winged feet, covered with feathers.

While he was sleeping, Delilah cut his hair, and yet, Samson awakens with relief to a reality more benign than his terrible nightmare: baldness.

The bad thing about alcohol is it goes straight to my head, and finding nothing to stop it, keeps going until I myself begin to wonder, oh God, where, oh where can my head be?

I tell a friend about a dream I had with him in it. You'll have to explain the ending to me, he says, as if dreams had endings, as if I could be certain it's over.

The arrow shot from the accurate crossbow of William Tell splits in half the apple that is about to fall on Newton's head. Eve takes one half and offers the other to her partner, to the delight of the serpent. This is how the law of gravity never came to be formulated.

BONDAGE

Many prefer to be bound, and naturally, the kind of bondage varies depending on the resources of the aroused victim: from silk ties to blood ties. After all when you get down to it, nothing binds more than family responsibility—certainly the most expensive of all painful pleasures.

SADISTS

For those who take pleasure in the suffering or humiliation of others, a combination of gratifying stimulations are recommended, of which certain TV shows are not excluded.

CUTTING COSTS

Some masochists relish the thought that others witness their humiliation. Those who have the means hire two or more girls. But for the filthy rich, a stadium may be rented with five thousand extras. (It's rumored the spectators are sadists who are charged admission.)

SOPHISTICATION

For the most sophisticated (but let's admit it's a very expensive perversion), Madam is willing to provide the client with the services of his own wife.

NEAT FREAKS

Neat freaks wear many articles of clothing and take them off slowly. By the end of the first year, they've finally removed their hats and socks and placed them carefully on a chair. When naked at last, they look at their partner with some disappointment, and a few demand she be exchanged for a younger woman. Like all the rest, they pay by the hour.

THE PAINTED LADIES

The ladies paint themselves before night falls. They paint their eyes, nose, arms, toes, and the crease behind their knees. They paint themselves with imported makeup, acrylics, with pencils and brushes. By dawn, they have vanished. With each passing hour and each man, they fade away.

GOLEM AND RABBI I.

Many kabbalists were capable of making a Golem, but not all could make their Golem obey them. The story is told of a rebellious Golem, shaped by a certain rabbi in his own image and likeness, who exploiting their remarkable resemblance, took the place of his Creator. This true story is completely unknown because no one could tell the difference, except for the rabbi's happy wife, who chose not to comment.

DEAD END CLUE

Couldn't it be dangerous to follow the trail of stains? How can we be sure they lead to the corpse, and not the murderer? (But the stains are ink blots guiding us to the word *end*.)

THE OLD MAN AND DEATH

A very old man bragged about knowing death because he was so much closer to her than others. Many asked him to describe death, and he'd invent an answer that would leave each one satisfied: it's like being in the womb, it's like a blind rhinoceros, it's like your grandma's kitchen. He'd say things like that and was revered for his words. Nevertheless, death had already paid him a visit and, unbeknownst to him, they've been together for a long time.

FATHER AND SON

He had a son who grew up to be just like him when he was that age. Despite his efforts to let his son catch up, the father couldn't help but stay ahead. Nevertheless, after a certain number of years, the advantage he had over his son began to slip, leaving him behind.

"Don't worry, Pop," his son would say to console him, "life isn't a race."

That's easy to say when you're winning.

TIME TRAVEL

Time travel's not only possible but also inescapable and never ending. Ever since I was born, I've done nothing but sail toward an abominable fate. What I'd like to do is stop, stay right here, which isn't too bad: throw out the anchor.

JUDGMENT DAY

Intensely engrossed in his favorite show, he fails to notice that the rest of the world has vanished around him, that the trumpets have sounded, and the Four Horsemen have spread their fury. He fails to notice that he has been judged once and for all, that having weighed his good and bad deeds, the faithful scale has tipped in his favor, and he remains now and forevermore, intensely engrossed in his favorite show, in Heaven.

MEDICAL ASSISTANCE

My wife, always so stubborn, Doctor. But she respects you. Convince her, please, to stay still, and not get up barefoot in the middle of the night, and roll her eyes at the guests. Convince her, Doctor, she'll listen to you, that real corpses don't move or complain, or if they do, they're not really dead. But please, Doctor, help her make up her mind once and for all.

PROPHETS AND CATASTROPHES IV

They banished him from the city when his prophecy came true. He had predicted abundance, good harvests, happiness. Only then did he understand that people take all the credit for their good fortune but won't own up to their rotten luck. Since then, he only foretells calamities. He gets paid even more when they don't come to pass.

FOR LACK OF PROOF

Enormous leaps, sixty or ninety feet high, in which I soar above the tree tops, and yet that's all they are, leaps: the devastating proof that I can't fly.

CULTURAL TABOO

Due to some cultural taboo we have yet to understand, the natives refuse to accept the collaboration of our scientists to determine why, time and time again, the harvest of humans goes to waste in those cultivated fields they call cemeteries. When it would be so easy to make them bear fruit!

THE MAGICIAN WHO BELIEVES IN MAGIC

The magician knows all his tricks and yet he believes in his own magic so much that he's tried to fly many times. With several broken bones, but with his enthusiasm still intact, he knows that just being alive is a miracle and gladly takes credit for it.

THE UNSURPASSABLE ART OF MA LIANG

Ma Liang was a legendary Chinese painter whose imitation of the world was so perfect he could transform it into reality with the final stroke of his brush. An emperor, who demanded he paint the ocean, drowned in it, along with his entire court.

To surpass the art of Ma Liang, the West invented photography, and later movies, in which the dead survive, repeating the same acts over and over again, as in any other Hell.

BAD ADVICE

Following the sorcerer's advice, he carved a wooden figure in the exact image of his enemy and burned it in a field, at night, under the moon. Attracted by the glow of the bonfire, his enemy found him and killed him with one thrust of his spear.

EXCESSES OF PASSION

We loved each other madly, fusing our bodies in one. Now only our ID's prove we were once two, and yet we still have challenges to face; the tax forms, the relatives, the distressing fact that we don't have as much in common as we thought.

FLIGHT OF FREEDOM

I opened his cage and threw him from the tower window toward life. Fly! I told him. But natural born prisoners fear freedom. I was reminded of that by his final desperate bark.

HIS WIDOW AND HIS VOICE

From the pipes there arose a loud and sad noise, which she believed to be the voice of her dead husband. All of the pipes make noise, her friends argued. His spirit reveals itself in all of the pipes, she said. All of the pipes made noise when he was with us, her friends insisted. But only now do they speak to me of love, she replied.

IN THE WHEELCHAIR

Aunt Petra pretends to be paralyzed so she can live in her wheelchair, wrapped in a plaid blanket that hides her goat hoofs, her fish tail, her snake bottom. My cousins and I took the blanket off Aunt Petra while she was sleeping, and we saw the two skinny little child legs she puts on whenever she takes a nap.

FORGETFULNESS

To conceal he no longer remembers them, he avoids using their names. To conceal he no longer recognizes their faces, he treats men as if they were close friends. He observes others constantly and imitates their gestures and actions with a one-second delay. His world is fragile, strange, and lonely, but on the other hand, it has its advantages. No one else can sleep each night with a different woman who claims to have been married to him for twenty years.

ONE TIME ONLY

Zeus, transformed into a swan, seduces Leda.

Afterwards, more than four swans dead from asphyxiation since that instant of perfect pleasure, of divine bliss that Leda insists on recreating in vain.

IMPOSSIBLE TO LIVE WITH

The man paints well, there's no question about that, but he drinks a lot of absinthe, is violent, moody, and downright impossible to live with. Taking extreme measures, with one decisive slash, the ear takes definite leave of Van Gogh.

VAN GOGH II

They say Van Gogh cut off his ear for a prostitute. Others affirm it happened in a fight with Gauguin. Some scientists insist he did it because he suffered from Ménière's Syndrome and was tormented by the ringing in his ears. I was a little girl, and I saw him with my own eyes, and I can assure you he did it for this, to use it as a seed, said the ancient woman from Arles, pointing with pride to the tree laden with spiral shaped fruit, like soft hairy snails.

SEAGULL TIME

The seagulls have arrived, the tourists have gone away with the last rays of sun, and on the beach lies debris, the remains of the day: disposable cups, plastic bags, empty cans, capless tubes of suntan lotion, broken barrettes, napkins smeared with mustard or mayonnaise, and a beautiful woman, lying face up, forgotten by someone who left her behind on the sand, a little sad because she knows she'll soon be washed away by the waves.

THE MAN WITHOUT A CHILDHOOD

That man was never a boy, people used to say, and they were right. The result of a prolonged pregnancy, he was born at the age of twenty-five, after a difficult and fatal labor.

POETS

Stranded on this distant land where spaceships don't pass nor ever will, lost on this speck of sand far from all the commercial routes of the universe, I'm condemned to share the intrinsic solitude of its inhabitants, people incapable of communicating with a tool less unwieldy and impenetrable than language. I use it to send coded messages that only other castaways, those they call poets, can understand.

ERIC JAROSINSKI

Q: The form of your aphorisms is unique, short sequences of laconic phrases or sentences. How did you arrive at this form, and what about it appeals to you?

A: Short answer: out of necessity. Once I start writing a full sentence or two, I start to panic a little and the writing tends to fall apart. I'd like that to change, but so far it has not. As to the general tone: I was once told that I write parodies of aphorisms, and that sounds about right. I dislike the form's traditional note of authority. That's why I often grossly exaggerate any claim an aphorism might have to truth. Extreme brevity helps with that. At the same time I'm discounting what I have to say, however, I also want to say it. And believe it's worth saying. But I want the reader to know that I'm well aware that the world couldn't care less about my opinion on the matter. In sum, I suppose you could say form began by following function. Then unfollowing it. Blocking it. And it's probably burning its house down at this very moment.

.
.
.

#KEEPITSIMPLE

Only two problems with the world today.

The world.

And 2. Today.

Three, if you count tomorrow.

#THEFINEPRINT

Someday we will read the terms.

We will read the conditions.

We will wonder why we ever agreed to them.

And check yes.

#BITTERSCHÖN

It's not the depression.

It's the anxiety.

The thought of waking up some morning.
Alone.

With nothing left to fear.

#AUTOGENESIS

In the beginning:

There was the word.

And it was autocorrected.

To world.

#HOWTOFINDHAPPINESS

Think of where you last saw it.

See if it's still there.

If it's not, ask yourself why it left.

If it is, ask yourself why you didn't stay.

#FORMULAIC

Comedy = tragedy + time.

Dark comedy = tragedy + time + tragedy.

German comedy = tragedy + time − comedy.

Dark German Comedy = Greek tragedy.

#MIXEDRECEPTION

The good news:

Technology has brought us closer together.

The bad news:

Please see above.

#GENRETROUBLE

The aphorism:

Philosophy's ship in literature's bottle.

The epigram:

Literature's hole in philosophy's bucket.

#THISISNOTAJOKE

Magritte walks into a bar.

Smoking a pipe.

Sits down next to Freud.

Smoking a phallus.

#WELTANSCHAUUNG

A gentle reminder:

To be thankful for the big things.

To fetishize the little things.

And to gently Photoshop everything in between.

#PISTOLSORSABERS

At least there are the radicals.

Always there to challenge our worldview.

To a bloody duel. At dawn.

Followed by brunch.

#NEGATIONOFTHENEGATION

No, friends.

You don't have to suffer from false consciousness –

To be a bourgeois academic Marxist.

But it helps.

#GLOATINGSIGNIFIERS

The poets remember it.

A time when words meant something.

Something important.

For which there are no words.

#UTOPIANPROJECTS

Say no to a nowhere.

And yes to a somewhere.

Somewhere else.

In the middle of nowhere.

#JUSTLIKEME

Yes, we'll say.

Social media.

It's when our friends left our lives.

And moved into our phones.

GEORGE MURRAY

Q: **You've published more poetry books than aphorism books, so I'm assuming -- always dangerous -- that you may see yourself as a poet who sometimes write aphorisms rather than the other way around. How do you know when it's an aphorism that's coming, rather than a poem? Are they rooted in different circumstances, attitudes, emotional or cognitive states?**

A: I started as a poet and only came to aphorisms in 2008 or so at the suggestion of James Richardson, who admired the closing couplets in a book of my sonnets. I realized then that many of the unused "lines of poetry" in my notebooks were in fact aphorisms. Since the discovery of that first cache of complete aphorisms, I've found that poetry and aphorisms happen alongside one another in my daily work. I never know which they are until I examine them later. An idea may present itself as either a line of poetry, needing other lines of poetry around it to feel complete, or it may present itself as a complete aphorism.

I sometimes call aphorisms "poems without all the poetry getting in the way." For me, the line that arrives whole, needing nothing else added to make a complete poetic/philosophical/humourous statement becomes an aphorism. The circumstance, attitudes, and emotional/cognitive states are all virtually the same, or at least blended into one another, so I don't think of the writing of poetry and aphorisms as separate acts. I suppose the reason I have so many more books of poems is pretty practical: in my experience it takes about 30 poems to make a poetry book, whereas it takes about 450 aphorisms to make an aphorisms collection—and I can spend just as much time on each individual piece.

⋮

Events without consequence are called *acts*; events with consequence are called *memories*.

Stupidity is society's shitty weather: there's no use complaining about it.

Those who have least are most qualified to define *enough*.

The man standing at the dead end need only turn around to see the road go on.

History and elegy are only separated by one's proximity to events.

You don't own privacy, you share it.

When your worst enemy is circumstance, your best friend is chance.

Yes may grow from maybe, but maybe seldom grows from no.

Being lost is achieved only by those who think they deserve to know where things are.

Nude calls for a photograph; naked, the police.

Cliché was once wisdom, but then everyone found out.

Lies are like water: sustaining in small amounts, dangerous in volume.

Life is water; death the bottom of a hill.

You need only change your shoes to change your point of view.

If God is a compass, religion is the room in which it has been lost.

Each human is like a hotel room: all basically the same layout.

The secret no one wants to know isn't a secret.

Gods anger us by not being gods; parents also.

Novelists are students of what it means to be people; poets are students of what it means to be me.

Time knows how to heal all wounds because time inflicted them.

If is the smallest unit of hope.

Love: the soul's milk; lust: its coffee.

The same tree that provides shelter during the storm continues to drip on those beneath it long after the storm ends.

Mediocrity does more to stifle brilliance than idiocy ever could.

Leaders are seldom the first to arrive.

Screams don't have accents.

I'm no narcissist, but the guy in the mirror sure is.

Epiphany is the third ball thrown towards the hands that have already caught one each.

Friends are made of unpaid debts; and unmade by the same.

Unfinished endeavours can wait longer than you.

The pebble is harder to break than the rock.

Every year I am finally old enough to handle last year's problems.

Everything in the universe is either me or not me.

Idealism in children almost always looks ugly, just like the lack of it in adults.

Thought is like water: deadly when there is too little and dangerous when there's too much.

Words work like feathers: each beautiful on its own, but only able to fly when put together.

Memory is foggy where forgetting is clear.

The poor act as custodians of styles that haven't yet come back around again.

The longest journey also ends with a single step.

YAHIA LABABIDI

SF: Have your aphorisms changed in the years since you first began to write them?

YL: A funny thing happened. Just as my aphorisms were beginning to gain traction in the world, I stopped writing them. When I spoke of them, I felt like an imposter. I no longer knew where they came from. I had no idea where they'd gone. I'd begun writing them as a late teen and defined them to myself as 'what is worth quoting from the soul's dialogue with itself.' Now when I listened for them, I heard nothing. Something had shifted within me. My soul was being rewritten and readied for fresh utterance.

It was more than a decade before the aphorisms returned, and they had changed, in the interim, as had I, as had the times, and the prevailing tastes. I allowed myself new liberties. The aphorisms need not be declarative or neat or strictly philosophical, because neither was I. They might be fragmentary, poetic and occupied with the mysterious life of the spirit.

We kneel in stages. Two and a half decades ago, a mighty spirit whispered to me and rearranged my days. Drink, it said, of solitude; taste of silence. I did as I was told and it made me a writer of aphorisms. Now, it's back again with grander designs to transform my being. Renounce, it insists, word games, and world games. I have no choice but to submit, bow, and write what I am told.

⋮

You can't bury pain
and not expect it
to grow roots.

All who are tormented by an Ideal must learn to make an ally of failure.

If Love were not always a step ahead, how would it ensure that we kept up the chase?

Every Messiah is reluctant—at least, initially.

Poor rational mind, it would sooner accept a believable lie than an incredible truth.

Mind is the handrail we clutch in the dark, for fear of falling. Yet, it's precisely what trips us—where the stairs diverge.

There are many ways to donate blood, writing is one.

We must try not to take our fight with ourselves out into the world.

As we make peace with ourselves, we become more tolerant of our faults—
in others.

In our inverted era, the Love that dare not speak its name is Divine.

Where there are demons, there is something precious worth fighting for.

For the sake of a good line, a poet, like a comedian, must be willing to risk
everything.

If you wish to be heard, speak gently. The same holds true in speaking to
ourselves.

Unlike prose, poetry can keep its secrets.

Aphorisms respect the wisdom of silence by disturbing it, briefly.

An apocalyptic viewpoint is a veiled death wish.

Compassion is to recognize the role we play in the creation of our enemy.

Cynics are in need of constant reassurance; first, that their worst doubts about humanity are true and then, of course, that they are not.

Numbness is a spiritual malady, true detachment its opposite.

To acquire a third eye, one cannot blink.

What we refer to as "the real world" is often our failure of imagination.

ELISA GABBERT

Q: You've published two books of poetry, but *The Self Unstable* was marketed as "Essay/Literature"—do you think the genre label affects how people read the collection?

A: Yes, in retrospect I think it does. "Prose poetry" is kind of a bullshit category, since in reality the only thing that makes poetry *poetry* is that it isn't prose—prose can do anything poetry can do except be in lines. We wouldn't even need the word "prose" if we didn't have poetry!

It's kind of amazing when you think about it: By organizing text into lines, poets magically make the text much more difficult for most people to read and comprehend. It's as though the extra white space on the page somehow creates complexity—as though the absence of meaning to the right of the line (seriously, there's nothing there) creates a void that, in horror vacui, the mind tries and fails to fill. Perhaps this is why, by virtue of being prose and not poetry, *The Self Unstable* has far outsold my other two books.

.
.
.

Memory comes first, then identity shortly after, at age 7 or 8. I wanted to be pretty, and now I am. Did wishing make it so? That I am *I* is less shocking than its opposite, that you are *you*. One day in my 20s, sitting in a cold car, I realized the self is universal, there is only one *I*—again, the thought arrives, but no longer seems profound.

Animals can think about thinking, a grand failure of evolution. The best experiences involve no thinking at all, much less self-reference, much less an endless/strange loop. Whatever you do, don't start thinking about thinking.

I saw a figure from a distance and thought it was me. I drank from the opposite side of a glass. If you can't describe how you feel to yourself, you can't be sure what you're feeling—or that you feel at all. Consciousness as unreliable narrator. The self is a play that you watch from the audience— you affect it, but you can't control it.

One of my earliest memories is of drinking a Coke and feeling like I'd finally arrived. No experience is complete until I narrate it to myself. The algorithm is simple; it's the input that's random. The best way to speed-read is to turn off your inner voice, your mind-brain duality.

If you suspect that your child is a genius, observe it carefully. Does it use abstract logic for problem solving and have a high curiosity level, an extraordinary memory, a vivid imagination, and an excellent sense of humor? These signs are often seen in geniuses. Always keep a control child nearby for comparison. I strongly suspect that I was the control child. My brother convinced me I wanted to be a boy. Or, because of my brother, I wanted to be a boy.

There's no respect without fear, but there is fear without respect. This is another way of saying that fear is everywhere, which is why it's so scary. No aspect of my life is free of marketing. We were wrong about the infinite possibilities. You have to choose between the pure idea and the blaze orange tree.

Most days we don't think about the war. We don't watch the news. What we don't know might hurt us, but we're protective of our pain. The life of the mind: Life is in our minds, and the news is outside. Life is tragic in real time, but the memories are farcical. What good does it do to feel the same things over and over, to rehearse the same pains? Where are the clouds of the mind? Where is the play within the play?

The last day of my 29th year, I woke up crying. "Despite myself." Youth is wasted, full stop. We trade awe for regret, beauty for truth. I'll remember forever how Brandon Shimoda threw his half-eaten ice cream cone in the trash: "This is *boring*." Awe is nothing like shock. Time moves so fast I want it to move faster, make memories of you.

The word *sexy* is sexy. That's how culture works. All language is descriptive. If you're not "trying too hard" you're trying hard not to. Irony is seen as a filter on sincerity; in truth both irony and sincerity are filters. In its pure form the data is too powerful.

They slowed down Beethoven's *Ninth Symphony* so it stretched over 24 hours. The effect was of a continual climbing, with no resolution—just an ever-building terror, the slowest imaginable scream. In a state of heightened time, everything reduces to fear, a sublime fear. If life has any meaning, it comes at the end.

A visitor from the past would look around and mainly see an absence of hats. The primary purpose of fashion is to signal in-group conformism. If everyone walked around naked, it would be difficult to spot our natural allies. We grow attached to our enemies. We would rather they not apologize, which would obviate the reason to hate them.

Girls want to be beautiful. Boys want to be powerful. In other words, everyone wants to be powerful. The appeal of Houdini and lingerie is the same: The more straps you wear, the nakeder you look. The only natural responses to vulnerability are love and violence.

When you suspect someone is in love with you, you begin to treat them with contempt. Cruelty is justified, even an obligation. You engage in the feminism of rejecting your beauty. Nevertheless, you hope to remain attractive. In fact, you become more so. Men test the limits of your capacity for cruelty, follow you into bars.

My ex read about a woman who believed she was having orgasms, until she finally had a "real" one. He suggested my orgasms might not be real. What an odd way to undercut me, since he was the one providing them. Is it even possible to have an imaginary orgasm? If you believe you are happy, aren't you, for all intents and purposes, happy? Don't you always feel the way you feel?

Sexual tension must culminate or deteriorate; thus all passionate friendships end with resentment. Be careful what you do "with abandonment." In fantasies of sudden death, one's enemies are finally sorry; this only endears them to the fantasizer. Be careful what you wish for, in that it tells you what you want.

Koans are used to provoke "the great doubt." Contentment isn't happiness. I told a student that desire comes from boredom. But I seek out desire, so why do I fear boredom? Maybe emotions *are* ideas. I believe in the end of history illusion, but I also believe in the end of history, the failure of all imagination. The future isn't anywhere, so we can never get there. We can only disappear.

STEPHEN DOBYNS

Q: Is there a single event or circumstance in your life that led you to become a poet?

A: It would be hard to say that some particular event led me to becoming a poet, but it is very clear what led me to loving books. My mother read to me a great deal. In addition, I had two aunts whose fiancés were off in the Navy (this was during WWII) and who were happy to read to an affectionate and attentive child. We lived in Chatham, NJ, and had a brown armchair big enough to accommodate me and my mother, or one of my aunts. So, between the ages of three and five I heard a lot of Beatrix Potter and Mother Goose, and then Rudyard Kipling's *Just So Stories* and *The Jungle Book*, and books that had been my mother's books—*Black Beauty* and *Little Lord Fauntleroy*, George MacDonald's *The Princess and the Goblin*, *The Princess and Curdie* and *At the Back of the North Wind*. Many, many books that I heard over and over. But the book that I kept coming back to was Robert Louis Stevenson's *A Child's Garden of Verses*, and so if any particular book influenced me it was that one, and I still repeat several of those poems to myself, and I read them to my own children.

Well, the war came to an end and my aunts married and moved away. I was also getting bigger. I remember the disappointment I felt when I grew too big to fit comfortably next to my mother or one of my aunts in the big brown chair, to lose that affectionate and edifying warmth. But my mother continued to read to me all through grade school, especially when I was sick, and in all of that I feel myself very fortunate. But whether or not that led me to becoming a poet I cannot tell.

⋮

Age: not what you were promised.

Ambition: ladder made from the backs of others.

Ambivalence: cowardice in the abstract.

Articulate: says what you wish to hear.

Beauty: reason's saboteur.

Boredom: a lack of diversion making one focus on what exists.

Bric-a-brac: the cherished objects of another's aesthetic.

Camouflage: smiles.

Candid: strategy for introducing an untruth.

Certainty: doubt's vestibule.

Charm: when you can't be good.

Clothing: another of anxiety's disguises.

Compliment: precedes a request.

Concession: the crumb tossed to another's assertion.

Contempt: you have nothing he wants.

Corpse: lately full of plans.

Cynicism: when truth no longer helps.

Definition: pup tent in bewilderment's snowstorm.

Dependable: still lends you money.

Diabolic: the wish to unsettle the seemingly fixed.

Dignity: elevator shoes.

Duty: tends to others' business before his own.

Ego: doorman of a building rising into the fog.

Elsewhere: where the good things happen.

Enough: what others have.

Fame: a longer echo. There, it's gone.

Fashion: the skeleton's gossamer boa.

Fear: premortem coffin.

Flattery: someone's insincere disclosure of your personal truth.

Forbearance: what he calls his cowardice.

Forgive: to delay retribution.

Fortitude: stubbornness in the face of evidence.

Friend: the one who believes the lies you tell about yourself and whose lies you choose to believe.

Fun: self-forgetting.

Gibe: heart dart.

Guest: your temporary better self.

Guilt: between the pleasure and the forgetting.

Hate: the heart's clenched muscle.

Idealist: rainbow peddler.

Insufficient: all that happened today.

Interminable: the time between the sweet talk and the payoff.

Isolation: afraid of loving back.

Jewelry: outer proof of inner value.

Judgmental: malice masked as the well-meant.

Keepsakes: the junk tossed out by your heirs.

Language: thought's shadow.

Laughter: the grease between you and the world.

Lavish: praise given to the undeserving.

Libel: someone calling you what you secretly call yourself.

Life: your stretch of river.

Lobotomy: on most people the scars don't show.

Love: where I erase myself.

Martyr: prefers the fame of his defeats.

Mystery: what language seeks to conceal.

Nationalism: a chip on the border.

Patience: the open door that allows the world to enter.

Peace: to be concerned no longer.

Pessimist: lacks the gift of self-deception.

Pragmatist: makes beauty ride in back.

Prejudice: hostility directed at another for not being one's self.

Quarrelsome: would have you bear the burden of his disappointment.

Revenge: when you can't win.

Revisionism: the step before the memoir.

Safety: nothing left to surrender.

Scribbler: uses a pen to polish his excuses.

Self: smoke and cobweb infrastructure.

Self-analysis: blind man drawing a dog.

Silence: no moon and the owl glides over the meadow.

Sleep: practicing to get it right.

Sophistication: cynicism tinseled with charm.

Splurge: to validate oneself through excess.

Sufficiency: an existential condition experienced by others.

Symbiosis: I like your poems, too.

Tenure: the excuse to strip off your falsies and corset.

Text: is to poem what biped is to sexpot.

Tradition: error's cherished accumulation.

Tragedy: the boss spilled his soup.

Truth: the province of the loud.

Utopian: no dream too big.

Vamp: salt dressed as sugar.

Wealth: the trouble that makes it better.

Weapon: resentments rigidified.

Winner: future loser.

Wish: when now isn't enough.

Xenophobe: barbed-wire-enthusiast.

Yesterday: the Almost preceding today's Not Quite.

You: proof of not me.

Your imperfections: what makes the water sparkle at sunset.

Youth: ignorance in a gift box.

Zany: the yet to be accepted by common consensus.

Zeal: untroubled by pros and cons.

Zealot: no cost too high.

Zero: waits while all the rest is lost.

DANIEL LIEBERT

"One man alone is too much for one man alone."
ANTONIO PORCHIA

Q: Your newer aphorisms have a somewhat darker tone than those before. How might you explain this?

A: Inspired by the Antonio Porchia quote above, I have put aside 'wit and word games' for awhile and asked myself the question: "Can the writing of aphorisms be a profoundly serious activity in my life?"

The subject of these aphorisms is 'one man alone'—myself. I stripped down to my 'existential skivvies' to write these; wrestled out the half-truths and scoured away easy answers. I wrote out of faith that a man is given an essential voice that can tell HIM essential things.

If nothing else, I hope to have captured the 'too-much-ness' of a man alone. We are all of us, such intrinsically lovely, *overwhelmed* creatures.

⋮

A man's life is made from what is at hand.

My greatest mistake: not asking more of those I loved.

Each worthless thing is worthless in its own way.

Lust becomes nothing, not even loneliness.

When I fear for tomorrow, I hardly even want today.

Love says *go with me*, even God's love says this.

I hoarded myself in you, yet you leave with nothing.

I am my own tree of forbidden knowledge.

Stones are pieces of time.

You charm me with the unreality I gave to you.

Mayflies live one day; for millions of years it has been so.

A tree is memory: sapling becomes heartwood.

Life is given to us whole, taken from us piecemeal.

Insomnia: yesterday's man refuses to die.

My aging is *mine* – I had not expected that boon.

All I ever really knew of you was you with me.

What I love, I don't love today.

There are chords within silence; harmonized stillnesses.

I will die where I was born, *in media res.*

From fear of being used, I became useless.

Here evokes infinite elsewheres.

Waking in the dark: life's mysterious *momentum*.

My love-life is over; this is my kindness-life.

Alone, I am neither young nor old—I am alone.

Not even a hand-hold; a mere breath-hold in this world, is all.

A meditation must exclude that which would end it.

Shame can live for years on its own excrement.

Life is interesting to itself—even for a gnat.

You would trade *your* joys for other joys?—that is so sad.

What is best in me is not mine, I belong to it.

My secrets have secrets from me.

Life is of infinite particular value.

I want to be caused by beauty I have made.

To have had a destiny—how I would have loved that!

I am the aging curator of my lusts.

Old Age: ever slighter gestures on a shrinking stage.

I'm just a tourist at the end of his tourism.

Now is ravenous, insatiable.

One's bank account of silence: deposits, withdrawals.

The hand: such a clumsy courier of touch.

Naked beside you, my body is pure *wanting to say*.

Death is in me like rust is in iron.

To be old in this old, old world!

My life, a monologue near a body.

I lie and lie and yet truth stays true in me.

I don't want what I need—I hate what I need.

Even if I have nothing, it is a God-given nothing.

The past is not behind us, it is trodden underfoot.

My last, desperate trick: to show her my empty bag of tricks.

My father died—how terrible that must have been for me.

Love nuances the heart, hate makes us crude.

Our shrinking love intensified like a doomed star.

What I know becomes what I didn't do.

God can be anything. Tonight, God is nothing.

The littleness of life is compounded daily.

Some men are crazy drunk on rotgut sobriety.

My past is the past of everything.

Spoken words enter the flow of time; thoughts hover like mist.

A blade of grass hyphenates earth to sky.

The fire in me does not fear fire.

A life of momentous indecisions.

My father is gone, text and lacunae both.

Eyes closed, I see the dark, rich gravy of self.

MARGARET CHULA

Q: What are some challenges of working in such an exacting form as the haiku?

A: I've spent thirty-seven years trying to convince people that just because a poem is written in three lines with a 5-7-5 syllable count doesn't make it a haiku—unless you're writing in Japanese.

The challenge of this shortest poetic form is to convey your insight through sensory images and suggestion—not to count syllables. Choose strong verbs and limit your use of adjectives. Think about a scroll painting surrounded by white space, and allow room for your readers to fill in their own experience.

Like Japanese haiku, English-language haiku are written in present tense (in the moment) and most have a seasonal word (*kigo*) to show a connection with nature. Most challenging—and exciting—is the juxtaposition between two seemingly unrelated things. This "turn" occurs after the first or second line and brings about a surprise, or "aha." The most memorable haiku leave us with new way of looking at the ordinary and a reminder of how we are interconnected with nature.

:

sultry afternoon
in Grandma's junk mail
Frederick's of Hollywood

Tokyo vending machine—
　the long line
　　behind the foreigner

restless autumn sea
remnants of Fukushima
arrive at our shores

winter dusk
my grief released
from the crow's throat

at a stranger's grave
I rearrange
the plastic flowers

condolence cards
filling the living room
with old friends

after you're gone
all my squash plants
still putting out blossoms

alone at midnight
and the fire's gone out
winter rain

cocktail hour
honeybees buzz
the tips of the mint

Mother's Day—
before her children arrive
she adjusts her wig

winter evening
a stray dog barks
to his echo

MICHAEL THEUNE
AND AUSTIN SMITH

Q: Describe your collaborative project writing haiku, or more specifically death poems, despite the fact that you don't seem to be—knock wood—facing imminent death.

A: With the Midwestern death poems project, Austin and I are perpetrating a kind of open hoax: we've written these haiku (sometimes alone, sometimes together, sometimes we're each other's editor), but we like to suggest that, instead, we've found them scattered throughout the Midwest. We like to think (for we know there is) a deep genius in the Midwest (one that, alas, is not always successful in its battles against the dark forces of nationalistic politics…).

These haiku (for each of us, a beloved form) are the fragments and further confirmations of that genius: always thoughtful, often feeling, often funny. Additionally, we simply like to scatter our haiku in this way. It is only right. Haiku come to the poet as a kind of gift. (Given the nature of haiku, there is very little difference between finding one and actually writing one.) It is good, then, to give them away, as well, as completely as possible.

⋮

one more prayer and then
i'm done pressing buttons on
this broken remote

yadda
yadda
ya

dying, the cave
crumbles
into bats

the words skip the
words skip the words
skip the words

the janitor who
no longer
votes lowers the flag

my unread books,
like extra
tombstones

he can't even stand
to turn her old horse
shoes into a game

after, she brings
the letter
opener to her throat

hand print slowly
disappearing
from the stress ball

the young surgeon,
feeling his heartbeat
in the scalpel

cleaner than an autumn
moon: my doctor's reluctance
to make eye contact

my clarity your
confusion when you
put my glasses on

the coffin
pillow—
both sides cool

how long can she keep
bumping into you
before you take her hand?

her wet tissues—
could they be less
like cherry blossoms?

DAVID LAZAR

Q: The "Aphorisms" issue of the journal you edit, *Hotel Amerika*, was instrumental in bringing a lot of contemporary aphorists out of the closet. Is the aphorism a particularly appropriate form for the early 21st century? If so, why?

A: I appreciate the appreciation of our Aphorisms issue! It was startling, and wonderful, to see who was writing aphorisms and how the aphorism was being considered, reconfigured, sometimes deconstructed by contemporary writers. As a writer who teaches nonfiction literature, I had always worked the importance of the aphorism into my classes—the way it functions in the essay, as well as its place as form that stands alone in Marcus Aurelius, Vauvenargues, Chamfort, Wilde, Parker, etc.

And then I started writing my own, which are collected in my new book, *I'll Be Your Mirror: Essays and Aphorisms* with University of Nebraska Press. It occurred to me the perfect place and way to do that was on Twitter. It limits posts to 140 characters, perfect for the classic aphorisms (though some writers string the aphorism, or use strings of aphorisms, to almost prose poem length). The classic aphorism, though, is short, a sentence.

"Brevity," as Dorothy Parker writes, "is the soul of lingerie," and the aphorisms I like to write are in the lingerie-genre: brief, nocturnal, occasionally perverse, and always (hopefully) revealing something unexpected.

This age, of course, thrives on attenuation. What better a form for the age than the aphorism, one of the oldest forms, and perhaps the shortest. I always feel, however, l as though the aphorism is little form that could, but manages to continually fall under the radar. It punctuates the essay, it delights in ephemeral though occasionally brilliant lines on Twitter or Facebook, it slides into conversations unexpectedly…but all the more reasons for collections, anthologies. And for exploring ways to actually use the aphorism consciously as a creative form. In my new book, I have a section of aphorisms called "Mothers, etc" done in collaboration with the Canadian artist Heather Frise, surreal aphoristic meditations on iconic motherhood. In any case, in the age of the sound bite, attention *en passant*, reading on the fly, perhaps the aphorism will finally rise to its pithy apotheosis.

⋮

The city wants you to listen to yourself listening to it.

When asked for my street address I say, "I'm standing right here."

The apparition of these faces in the crowd, petals on a wet black cellphone.

I have a Walk/Don't Walk sign on my staircase to prevent accidents between floors.

In the city, the person who walks through a crowd crying creates silent havoc. Crying is a virus; you might catch it and die.

One of my earliest memories is riding the trolley in Brooklyn, which ended their run on October 31, 1956, 89 days before I was born.

It's always comforting to make your home feel home-like, a space that almost feels as though you live in it.

The body is a temple…of doom.

I like to surround myself with relics and artifacts of my childhood so my neuroses feel at home.

Self-epitaph: "He was, they say, not yet dead when he wrote this."

Walter Benjamin said astrology was for people who are afraid of taking control of their own fate. But what if you're afraid of people of who take control of their own fate?

You can't avoid grief; not so, love. Love is completely avoidable.

SAMI FEIRING

Q: What does it mean to you to be a writer of aphorisms, rather than other literary forms?

A: For me writing means exploring the world and the inner me. As an aphorist I consider myself an observer. The observer, though, often also becomes a critic when it is the senseless behavior of humans or the world that is under observation. An aphorism is a flying fish cavorting between philosophy and poetry. Therefore an aphorism must not only be a clever thought but has also to be composed in a stylized manner.

⋮

Knowledge is power, especially when you conceal it.

When politicians stumble, soldiers fall.

If nature could speak, it would remain silent.

Uniforms are body bags.

If all the world's a stage, where the hell is the prompter?

Today's Robin Hood takes from the man and gives to nature.

"God does not throw dice." He throws man.

When truth becomes unpleasant, just change the one who speaks.

A dissenting opinion requires a tie, a power of attorney or a thick wallet.

The politician lives in a fake marriage with truth, and keeps power as his lover.

Respect the book in your hand. It once was a tree in the forest.

A politician is two generations behind: He makes decisions for tomorrow based on yesterday's doctrines.

The wise statesman lets his people lead the way. That way, the enemy won't surprise from the front, or the friendly fire from behind.

The paradox of achieving change: the invidual's voice is not heard, the choir sings out of tune.

A soldier has no peace without war.

Sure the government clothes the poor: eye patches and straitjackets.

Your prison cell, my security net.

Treasure chests are Pandora's boxes.

The silence after the shout.

The stone in your shoe finds its way to your hand.

Thoughts come in different sizes: a needle sticks, a machete clears.

AARON HASPEL

Q: What drove you to aphorism?

A: It is a rather desperate measure, isn't it? In school you always had to show your work. Never mind the right answer, points off unless you explained how. Later on I wrote essays, and essays, too, require that your work be shown. A lifetime of showing my work has made me old, tired, and impatient. Aphorists do not show their work.

⋮

We despise capitalism, democracy, and technology not for giving us what we want, but for showing us what we want.

One reads so as not to believe everything one reads.

People say they can't draw when they mean they can't see, and that they can't write when they mean they can't think.

What we call maturity is mostly fatigue.

We say of indelible characters from life that they could be fictional; and from books, that they could be real.

A chief source of the world's ills is that it is run largely by people who did well in school.

In politics you can be right as long as you don't care if you win, or win as long as you don't care if you're right.

Few would deny that the earth was flat if it were a small inconvenience to maintain that it is round.

Abroad we make our soldiers pretend to be policemen, and at home we let our policemen pretend to be soldiers.

It is difficult, when you are poor and obscure, to persuade anyone of your indifference to wealth and fame.

Where books are burned, they are taken seriously.

It is the rare philosopher who notices how well most of the world gets on without philosophy.

If the object of desire is rich, we call it gold-digging; if handsome, lust; if clever, fascination; and if he has no discernible appeal, we call it love.

Education is free: credentials are expensive.

No universally acclaimed institution has a more dismal track record than marrying for love.

Revolutions spare nothing but the machinery of the state at which they are ostensibly directed.

First school spoils us for learning, then jobs spoil us for work.

Man is the only animal that cheats at solitaire.

A grudging willingness to admit error does not suffice; you have to cultivate a taste for it.

No-brainer, *n.* An idea that is extremely persuasive as long as you don't think about it.

Computers will never be intelligent because humans define intelligence as whatever they do better than computers.

When we can no longer tell ourselves that we are good, we tell ourselves that we are exceptional.

Shared antipathies are ties that bind.

First you do not write what you think, then you do not say what you think, and finally you do not think what you think.

One of truth's greatest enemies is collegiality.

When we are exhorted to be practical, realistic, or grown-up, it is always in service of something hideous.

Failure is always an option. Often it is the best option.

The people are flattered more obsequiously than the monarch ever was.

No government suppresses thought and speech as effectively as your friends and neighbors do.

The less you are contradicted, the stupider you become. The more powerful you become, the less you are contradicted.

The people never means quite all of them.

Today we hear silence as our ancestors heard music.

An electronic device that tracked your location at all times used to be a condition of parole.

You never violate your principles: you only discover that they are not what you thought they were.

Whatever you have done, you are the sort of person who would do that.

We wish, not to be understood, but to be misunderstood exactly as we misunderstand ourselves.

When God wants to punish you, He sends a person of bad character who shares all of your opinions.

S.D. CHROSTOWSKA

Q: As you are from Poland, I presume that English is not your first language. Yet your English prose is exquisitely concise and evocative. I am reminded of Nabokov and Conrad, who for their own reasons ended up writing in English, and are seen since as consummate stylists. If there were an ideal language for you to work in, or a hybrid language, what might that be?

A: My ideal language is *epitaphic*, a language of considerate brevity that honors the dead, their wish to be remembered. It is, at the same time, a language that is *posthumous*, freed from concerns over its timeliness or untimeliness and addressed to those who are still alive. As epitaphic, it is a language timeless enough to be carved in stone; as posthumous, it is impossible to write in while one is still alive. My ideal language is writing (in any language) that has these two characteristics. Writing done in this language is my inscription on the tomb of the past, but only as long as I am also already inside the tomb.

⋮

TRIPWIRE

The distance from a statement ringing true to being true is very small, and bisected by a tripwire.

PURSUIT OF IGNORANCE

Nothing so shows a man to be ignorant as the pursuit of absolute truth.

TAN LINES

On the outstretched arms of white beggars the sun marks the global colour line.

SORE SPOTS

The desperate pursuit of happiness is justified as long as suffering is guaranteed.

IMPOSSIBLE BUT NECESSARY

Even in us cynics, beauty and purity will always find a hiding place as long as we dwell on the world's ugliness and impurities.

IN BAD COMPANY

What is resentment if not the need for equality expressed in company that does not share this need?

A LA CHIENLIT!

As mortality goes the way of all flesh, the only death will be social, and nothing worse than it.

FALLS THE SHADOW

Going through life aware of omnipresent death is like lying on a beach with one's eyes closed, and knowing one is still there only by the chill of a shadow and the sand in one's mouth.

SAVE THE DATE

Some truths persist, others are of the moment and die with it. Those are the truths of fear, audacity, exuberance, fury, or ecstasy.

CANNON-FODDER

Grand statues of conquerors would sometimes be made of melted cannons captured from the losing side. The man-eating cannons would themselves become man-fodder. Justice history may lack, but not *poetic* justice.

EAT ME!

Every one of the gifts of history that one generation offers the next has a poisonous side it never advertises.

FIDGETY SITTERS

The past does not stand still, like the backdrop against which we gather to have our generational picture taken. How can it, if we cannot sit still in the present?

UNRECOGNIZED TWIN

Those who reject nostalgia reject also progress or change, of which nostalgia is the surest symptom and sign.

LOST & FOUND

Having nothing to lose is seen for what it is, an exaggeration. As long as life is lived, there will be something to lose, and loss of life guarantees no proportionate gain for the survivors.

DISPUTED INHERITANCE

The worm belongs to the earth alive. We, only dead.

FIRST THINGS FIRST

Having something to say is, first of all, having someone to speak to.

DEAD LETTERS

There always comes a time when a dear friend's silence can no longer be taken *personally*.

COMMON, SENSES OF

What is dismissed as common nonsense often makes uncommon sense.

CREDO

The aphorist: the houdini of reason.

ENDINGS

Can be eelusory.

RICHARD KOSTELANETZ

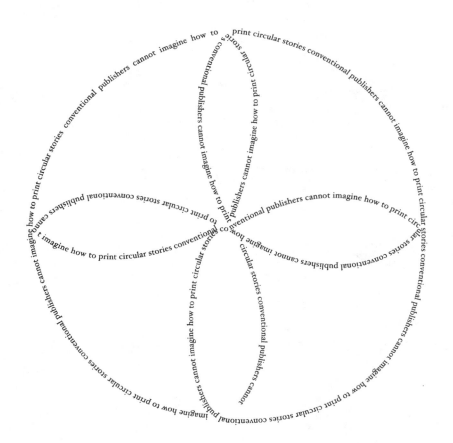

Disappointments reveal fresh truths.

"Self-improvement" is usually illusory.

Yes, no means no.

Aphorisms complete themselves.

Few statements become aphorisms.

"Weathermen" don't make weather.

Clothes hide truths.

Alcoholics can't relate naturally.

Heaven has other people.

"Theology" fakes comprehending mysteries.

Writers' writers write masterpieces.

Doubt belief in nothing.

No lie survives forever.

That that is is.

Worry inhibits clear thinking.

Higher truths are simple.

Power desensitizes.

Honest people appear opinionated.

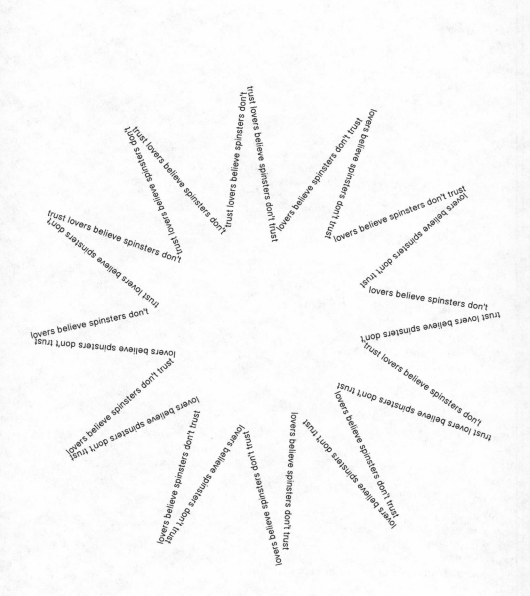

like boys who like girls like boys who like girls like boys who like girls like boys who like girls like boys who like girls like boys who like girls like boys who like girls like boys who like girls like boys who like girls like boys who like girls like boys who like girls like boys who like girls like boys who like girls like boys who like girls like boys who like girls like boys who like girls like boys who like girls like boys who like girls like boys who like

LILY AKERMAN

Q: You've written aphorisms, poems, and on a Fulbright award, lyrics for theater -- three forms of writing that imply three different mindsets. How do you decide which mindset, or which material, is best suited for which form?

A: An aphorism can't repeat or digress. It can't do horror. It can't take me to Hogwarts. Individuals like Harry Potter dissolve in aphorisms, usurped by general subjects like "he," "one," or "a stone." Anything historical, anything attached to a particular time and place, the aphorism doesn't do. Its limitations are also its latitudes. By eliminating breadth, the aphorism acquires depth. It looks so closely at a thing as to see through its exterior and into its essence. The individual is lost and the underlying human is found.

Dramatic forms take a difference course. Their subject is always, fundamentally, the body, because theater is expressed through bodies, among bodies. Bodies are subject to time, so a play is also about the passage of time. Its subjects, like people, can accrue experience, where the bodiless aphorism can't.

I write in different forms because each form is a terrain that guides my stream of thought in a particular direction. An aphorism lets me narrow in on the micro-moment, and a play sends me outward, spiraling through time and space. An aphorism transcends the body, and a play can't escape it. My hope is, somehow, to merge forms: to write a play that's a kind of embodied aphorism, to follow an impulse to its farthest implication, narrowing in by spiraling out, and experience two hours as a single, changing, instant.

⋮

I think therefore I think. I feel, therefore I am.

Every decision spawns a thousand fractal decisions. Even choosing carefully, I choose at random.

A gift is the freedom to take it for granted.

She rambles, and I don't listen. So from one narcissist another is born.

The original was also a translation.

The better I know one person, the better I know everyone.

He can't hear you over the noise in his skull.

When everyone's fucked, the cynic can say, *at least I didn't try*.

Kill the spider, breed flies.

The map's creases are another map.

He worries what other people think of him, so as not to imagine they don't think of him.

Many reasons are given to obscure the one.

The servant's the master at dealing with the master.

Advice, unsolicited, sounds like a threat.

Worry doesn't count as preparation.

Depth, a stack of surfaces.

My real secrets are the ones that I don't know.

In life's last act, the spine, slowly, bows.

A new moon is no moon.

The tree's shadow affirms the tree.

No one deserved anything, until one person got what he never deserved.
Then everyone deserved a little bit of that.

He must watch closely, to always be looking the other way.

Love dies in half-lives.

Facts we possess, knowledge we become.

The sunflower, intending nothing, tends to the light.

JOSÉ ANGEL ARAGUZ

Q: I know you are fond of the greguerías of Ramón Gómez de la Serna, and your own work shows affinities with his works, which are short like aphorisms but have a distinctly different flavor. Can you describe what it is about greguerías that you find attractive?

A: Ramón (as he preferred to be called) was steeped in surrealism, and through his writing he consistently sought to change how he thought, making associative leaps between things as if shuffling a set of tarot cards. For example, in the greguería that goes "Hablar por teléfono: fumar un pipa por el oído," the act of talking on the phone is connected with the image of smoking a pipe through one's ear.

Ramón defined the greguería as being made up of humor plus metaphor; in this example, juxtaposition awakens the logic-making engine of the reader's mind so that the humor and metaphor happen instantaneously through a sentence whose quick pacing is worthy of both playwright and stand-up comic. Ramón's constant reinvention and knack for fine-tuning the means of making sense of and from the world has inspired my own writing of what I term "lyric aphorisms."

If a poet's job is partly to see what they can get away with aesthetically, Ramón in his greguerías chooses instead to get (carried) away with himself. In *The Book of Flight* (Essay Press) as well as my current projects, I am guided by the same sense of unpacking a personal poetic sensibility in an accessible manner.

⋮

FROM *HEARTLINES*

If is the saddest word in the language, because whatever follows if does not exist.

Time is a road walked until familiar.

Want Ads: Paper and ink mix with oil in the skin, leave hands dark.

The centipede is a row of buttons trying to undo themselves.

At the wedding of cloud and wind, hail is the rice tossed down that makes us family.

The light bulb is an egg that hatches light.

The rain hits and hits, writing out its many names.

The sun after a storm handles each thing at once.

When you die, you go from being the hands on the clock to being the clock itself.

FROM *THE BOOK OF FLIGHT*

In the book of flight, the butterfly is a rumor.

The moth, a theologist.

In the book of flight, the mosquito embodies guilt, goes from body to body burdened with life.

⋮

In the book of flight, plastic bags are brought in to do the work of clouds.

Dead leaves rest in the margins.

Grass clippings, eyelashes, fingernails: errata in the book of flight.

⋮

Whatever wind has to do with the ways of shadows, mere editing in the book of flight.

In the book of flight, stray hairs line unjustified paragraphs.

The first drops of blood   from a fresh cut   cloud   in the book of flight.

The joke about dropping a penny from the top of a building (*imagine dropping a dollar*), the cost written in the book of flight.

Last words go buried at the bottom of the page as footnotes in the book of flight.

The ringer of bells marks the hour with his work, and the hour rings, takes its place, another page number in the book of flight.

Submission: I look at how small each work is and wonder if all the hours and rooms and whims can be traced in this, my print.

Workshop: One hears tale of a man presenting meat to his tribe, an act which means luck and a way with the hunt, and another talking over the fire, saying that it is not enough.

From a friend: *I just read the letter I wrote you a year ago but never sent. I would send it to you now, but I suddenly can't bear to part with it, haha.*

⋮

In daylight, the moth delivers its news absentmindedly.

Shaking newsprint wings, the moth flaps and unfolds its own story.

The moth thrashes in the corner, as if it would shake itself free of itself.

⋮

The moth flails like a kite at a funeral.

In the bread aisle, a moth like a label flying off with its expiration date.

Steal and *starve*, petals on the plant of need.

Spiritual, the fly lingers over what is left behind, iridescent at the wake.

The fly glints with what it knows.

Were the fly sun-colored, would it be such a bother?

.
.
.

The fly reads the air around it in earnest, dizzy with interest.

The fly, asking its question wherever it goes.

The fly follows honey, garbage, anything really, whose essence is strong.

.
.
.

The fly, inconsistent in its prayers.

The fly, eager to catch up on what he's missed.

There are those who read like flies, the words on the page lightly walked over.

⋮

What friends, these stars that start being visible slowly after sunset, small reminders of what is possible: light burning off only after one has lived.

The clouds speak of what was and how it held and can hold no more because of weather, and out of those fragments one makes out what one can and moves on.

No matter the distance, stars feel personal.

ASHLEIGH BRILLIANT

Q: Which writers influenced you most deeply?

A: For sheer stimulation and excitement, it was Jules Verne. For somber poetic expression: A.E. Housman. For actual effect upon my own life and behavior: Dale Carnegie and his *How to Win Friends and Influence People*.

Q: How would you characterize your relationship to your own writing?

A: Like most of us, I do different kinds of writing. To me, the most important is what I get paid for, which for many years has been mainly the 17-word epigrams which I publish on postcards and license for use on other products. I also do a weekly 750-word essay in a local paper, the *Montecito Journal*. But I wish I were more appreciated for my poetry, and have now been twice nominated for the distinguished position of Poet Laureate of Santa Barbara. Since writing is my only significant talent, I feel it embodies the best of me -- especially in my nine books of *Brilliant Thoughts*.

⋮

My mind is open, by appointment only.

If I didn't have most of my friends, I wouldn't have most of my problems.

You know I'll always help you if you need me, so please don't need me.

How tired I feel! I understood so much today.

Please don't hide your love for me so well.

It would be easier to play my part in life, if I had a copy of the script.

Why are there so many similarities between what I'm looking for and you?

Do your best to satisfy me -- that's all I ask of everybody.

Everybody is entitled to my opinion.

The longer I live, the less future there is to worry about.

I live in a world of my own, but visitors are always welcome.

The answer to your question is very simple: I don't know.

Wonderful!—You have some of my favorite problems.

If you learn one useless thing every day in a single year you'll learn 365 useless things.

The nicest part of a revolution comes afterwards, when they put the king's head back on.

I would like to say a word on behalf of oppressed people everywhere: Help!

I need to break loose, and find some more comfortable chains.

Make peace not noise.

I feel disillusioned—do you have any good new illusions?

A terrible thing has happened—I've lost my will to suffer.

You and I are both exactly alike, but there the resemblance ends.

Missing—presumed married.

Sometimes the best medicine is to stop taking something.

One is really the only number there is! All the other numbers are simply collections of ones.

You are only part of my problem—another part is me.

It may or may not be worthwhile, but it still has to be done.

I wish all the people who sincerely want to help me could agree with each other.

Tempt me again, before my resistance builds back up.

What causes the mysterious death of everybody?

Mine is the cup of contentment with the crack in it.

Be careful, or you'll fall into a category!

IRENA KARAFILLY

Q: You write with exquisite clarity about "difficult" topics and feelings: error, guilt, inadequacy, self-defense. Is there ever peace for a writer cursed with "too many insights"?

A: "The unexamined life is not worth living," Socrates famously said. I think the statement is debatable but, in any case, I don't believe anyone gets to choose whether to be an examiner or a non-examiner; so much depends on the circumstances of one's birth and upbringing. I was born in the Urals but crossed several borders while learning to walk, talk, read, and write. I do not identify with any religious or cultural group and think Diane Abbott was right in saying that, "Outsiders often have an insight that an insider doesn't quite have." In other words, being an outsider may actually be an asset if one's ambitions in life include being an aphorist.

But getting back to Socrates, I think that, for better and for worse, I belong in his camp, but I also believe that there is such a thing as too much examination, too much self-awareness, and that this may leave one hovering on the sidelines, observing human affairs with a somewhat jaundiced eye. So would I rather be a fish, Frank Sinatra? No, but I would love to swing on a star, and carry moonbeams home in a jar instead of polished pearls of dubious wisdom.

⋮

Nothing is more devastating than the certitude of men out to improve the world.

The only resolutions worth making are those you'll enjoy breaking.

Nothing perishes more quickly than gratitude.

For some people longing is a greater pleasure than pleasure.

You can truly forgive only what you yourself are capable of.

The road to hell is paved with too many insights.

Men love you when you forgive them more than their mother ever could.

No aphorist has ever been saved by the truth of his own utterances.

Death is much less frightening than pain because you don't have to live with it.

True suffering often makes people heroic; daily disappointment only makes them crabby.

Nothing makes a man want to get married more than the sight of a lovely woman about to marry someone else.

It's one thing to make a mistake, it's another to become wedded to it.

Heaven was invented in a desperate bid to keep human beings from going mad.

You don't have to be a writer to wish that life were just a very rough draft.

When you slam the door, it is not your anger that echoes but your own inadequacy.

A hero is a man who has learnt to keep all his fears locked up in one forbidden room.

People often stumble into the truth, but more often than not fail to recognize it.

Guilt is just a cheap ticket toward self-absolution.

We celebrate hard work, we admire intellect, but what we worship above all is the goddess of good fortune.

People who demand that everyone agree with them today are tomorrow's tyrants.

The natural impulse of human beings is to defend themselves, especially when their own conscience advises silence.

Nothing breeds spite faster than awareness of one's own guilt.

Do not expect reason to triumph when there is a compelling reason to pretend that it does not exist.

Evil is the most democratic of all pursuits.

Having your wings burnt by the sun doesn't mean you shouldn't fly at all.

Mothers are meant to warn, children to ignore; how else is the human species to grow and multiply?

Love
is a key you find
long before
you've got a door.

PATRICK CARR
AND CLAYTON LAMAR
@DOGSDOINGTHINGS

Q: How has collaboration shaped your writing?

A: Collaboration has been essential to @dogsdoingthings from the beginning. We can only think of this body of work as a dialogue and a continuing game. The game is possible because there are severe formal constraints: Twitter's 140 character limit, plus the demand that every tweet describe dogs doing things. Once we discovered the game, it was intuitive for us and became very generative. Our collaboration ensured @dogsdoingthings evolved over time.

We each surfaced material for these tweets and then found ways to iterate on it. We've mined images, tropes, literary texts, pop culture, and historical events again and again. From different iterations have come different arrangements of our material, creating (we like to think) different effects and resonances. The variety we have found given our game's limitations is owed to our collaboration.

Q: Why dogs?

A: Our form is small, but dogs are not. Dogs are all-encompassing: they generate a vast array of subject positions organized around a single metaphor. Dogs are hapless, dogs are degraded, but then again, dogs are triumphant, exalted, and worthy of love. Dogs are as keen and alert as they are idiotic and insensitive. Dogs are universal, dogs are fringe. Dogs are in your house. Dogs are everything.

:

Dogs assuring you that what seems like farce today will be remembered, as tragedy—when it repeats, again, as farce.

Dogs observing that hope is the thing with feathers and adding helpfully, "For example, dinosaurs had feathers."

Dogs rasping, "I am that I am?" and lighting a cigarette from a burning bush, adding "I haven't heard that name in years."

Dogs sighing at the end of a mental health day, "It didn't work."

Dogs wondering, "What happens to celebrities when they die?" and visiting a wax museum, realizing, "Oh."

Dogs digging your skeleton out of the rubble, wondering, "Were they human?" and making it jig like a puppet, adding, "Or were they dancers?"

Dogs shouting, "GO HOME—" and shoving all life on Earth out into the darkness of space, adding, "YOU'RE DRUNK."

Dogs proclaiming, "The world ends when I die," and staring contemplatively into the distance, reflecting, "Cool."

Dogs observing that existence precedes essence and then you're dead before you know it.

Dogs coming back from the dead and just rolling over, trying for another ten minutes.

Dogs observing that just because it makes you stronger doesn't mean it's not killing you.

Dogs observing at the end of a life in sin, "Oh, YEAH."

Dogs considering the world of sobriety and noting finally, "I don't get it."

Dogs reminding you that you will never be beset with this particular configuration of concerns and anxieties, ever again.

Dogs climbing onto dry land for the first time in the history of evolution and wondering aloud, "Is it too early to start drinking?"

Dogs confirming the existence of alien life and our corresponding need to sell shit to it.

Dogs observing at the end of a life lived in fear, "Well, gosh."

Dogs sitting at a disconnected computer keyboard, repeatedly punching the Escape key.

Dogs noting, "New year—" and exploding into two identical beings intoning in unison, "New me."

Dogs noting that in the long run we're all dead, but in the very long run, it's the short run.

Dogs gesturing grandly toward all existence, sighing, "Tragedy—" and pausing briefly before adding, "Plus time."

HART POMERANTZ

Q: You have written that "an aphorism is a joke that went to college." As someone who has worked as a comic writer with Woody Allen and Lorne Michaels, do you think the distinctions some experts make between aphorisms and jokes are important? Why or why not?

A: Not all aphorisms are jokes but of those that are funny, the aphorism is more laden with pith and substance, more sophisticated and seems to be teaching us something deeper than the joke.

Aphorisms can have no sense of humor at all but still impart some bit of wisdom, whereas a joke can deliver a laugh and yet impart little wisdom. A joke is just a sleight of mouth. Its *raison d'etre* is to create a laugh response only, whereas the funny aphorism serves two soups of the day. A joke also contains more aggression with its punch line, whereas an aphorism is more restrained.

So the answer seems to be that there are distinctions between the two. It must be remembered that a joke without the laugh is stillborn, whereas an aphorism without the laugh can live forever.

⋮

We carry out nature's plan in the mistaken belief that it is our own.

Culture is the clothing the instincts wear.

Religion says, "Love thy neighbor." I say move.

Society should be indicted for killing the child in all of us.

Nothing exceeds the speed of light save the speed of darkness.

What holds the void?

Monuments should be built before the holocausts, as a warning.

My OCD shrink will not see me on any day that begins with a "T".

For some, giving up, is the only giving they ever do.

Marriage is better than being single as it protects you from being rejected by a complete stranger.

Freedom diminishes *pro rata* with the number of pictures of the leader in the city square.

The legal costs of a successful appeal should be born by the judge that got it wrong in the court below.

Thank God cows and fish can't read menus.

He who is of two minds is not even of one.

We need dogs at airports that can sniff out ideologies

Is masochism simply a case of mistaken identity?

The clergy are like theater ushers, but without the flashlights.

Sixty is the new fifty-nine.

It is a shame that the only way we can recognize our dentist in public is by looking up his nose.

A free man has the choice as to which prison he will live his life in.

Are the other vowels upset at Y for not being able to make a commitment?

She suffered from the need of perfection in others.

One of the major consequences of conquering another country, is the loss of some very fine anthems.

It's difficult for the corpse to think outside the box.

MEG POKRASS

Q: There's a fierce emotional realism in your microfictions. Is it possible to maintain that intensity of energy in longer work?

A: It is certainly possible to create emotional urgency in longer works, but I myself can't do so with my own writing. That's why I love microfiction. My brain seems to communicate best in compressed bursts. To me, poetry is closer to microfiction than any other form.

⋮

COMPETITION

She let him make love to her the first night and he told her that he would do so every single night for the rest of her life. She let him make love to her the next night, but it had already become a contest in his mind about whether or not he could do it exactly as well as the night before. She let him make love to her the third night, but she was no longer there inside her body—she was watching from a safe distance, sitting next to the dog, catching her breath.

SCRABBLE

I'm seventeen in the hotel with my father in the suite and the TV on, his wine not chilled as he likes, eyelids already droopy and unforgiving. He wants to play Scrabble with me, it's the thing we do at night, but I want the man sitting alone in the lobby who'd looked at me with crackling eyes as though he were an eel. When my father finally falls asleep in his bathrobe and shorts I slide out to the red velvet lobby where he is waiting for me.

ON THE SAND

At the beach, our bellies love the hot sand so much we talk about everything. She still looks like a kid, though her voice is deep, and breasts have recently sprouted as if defying some long, internal fight. She talks about her dad, how he thinks she's *shit* now that she's given up becoming a track star—and when her eyes come to rest on my body, I run toward the ocean.

THE SUNSET DISTRICT

Out near the ocean where her dead marriage floated, she woke up in the living room sofa bed with the overweight cat on her head. The cat had been watching pigeons trying to nest on an unexposed slice of balcony. She could hear the husband up early, packing to visit his girlfriend in Chicago.

THE MAGICIAN'S ASSISTANT

The city smells salty, orange light sneaks around his shower-curtained window, cabs call like geese, or mothers of missing children.

"Break a leg tonight," he says, kisses my mouth.

UP IN ALASKA

Way up in Alaska I found the man who loved me, but he could no longer move his feet. I found him half-dead, staring up at the sky, looking for a helicopter. He turned his head and said to me "I am sad" and when he spit my name, it froze—but I understood it.

CELLULOSE PAJAMAS

I wash the dark green leaves carefully, softly, just for him, and will share them on the drive to the grocery store, wrap ourselves in their cool cellulose pajamas, tell each other in bird language again and again, why it was we grew too close.

TIME LADY

Sometimes when worrying about her family she searched for relief from "The Time Lady" a robotic-sounding clock-programmed telephone mother who said, "The time is…" as though she were really there inside the phone, and you could keep listening and she'd keep talking, and she was always right.

ERIC NELSON

Q: If I recall correctly, you consider your short works to be poems more than aphorisms. This is borne out by the line breaks each contains. What effect do you think the line break provides?

A: In my aphoristic poems, line breaks are mainly about timing. Comics and magicians say that in their work timing is everything. I think that's true with aphorisms, too. Whatever humor, misdirection, irony, or insight that my aphorisms contain is revealed incrementally, line by line.

For example, the ironic point of this poem—*The safer we make ourselves/ the more we find to fear*—is slightly delayed and slightly more emphatic by being presented in two short, concentrated lines, with the pause at the end of the first line setting up the reversal in the next line.

I like to think of each line as a fuse burning toward the verbal firecracker that, I hope, pops in the reader's mind. The danger, of course, is that fuses sometimes fizzle out before they reach the firecracker. But I don't like to think about that.

⋮

The gray brain wants everything
black or white.

Why oppose opposites?
A hammer pulls as well as drives.
Only what is buried grows.

There's no future in old age.
Except immortality.

Believe ghosts before angels.
Ghosts speak
from experience.

The safer we make ourselves
the more we find to fear.

Before the wheel—the basket.
Before the need to move,
the need to hold.

It's not the going home
that's hard.
It's the wanting to.

If you'll have chickens,
expect hawks.

There's a last time for everything.

The tall clock
in front of the funeral home
has stopped running.

Cars swerve to avoid
the old straw hat
lying in the street.

On the road, dead
baby birds, dead frogs, dead snakes—
the other signs of spring.

After the dog died,
the empty water bowl
was too heavy to pick up.

Some trees leaf out top down,
some bottom up. By summer
who knows which is which?

A thousand greens
Make the mountain's
Singular green.

Overcast all day—still
The sunflowers inch their great heads
East to west, tracking the sun.

On a dry turd
a Monarch rested, wings spread.

Bright autumn day—
the room darkens, leaf after leaf
landing on the skylight.

Day of cold gray rain—
I stop caring where mountains end
and fog begins.

The woods in winter—
all the leaves down, nothing hidden.
Except the trail.

All day and night snow fell and rose—
a foot before it stopped—a vast occurrence
without a sound.

His nature was to look down,
hers to look up.
They both loved mountains.

She wanted to be larger
than life. He,
larger than death.

Her mistake—believing him
when he swore
he was a terrible liar.

When he stopped trying too hard
to make her want him again,
she still didn't want him.

When he looked into her eyes
he saw the sky. That blue.
That far away.

HOLLY WOODWARD

Q: Do you work self-consciously, composing an aphorism and deciding how to revise it—or do they come to you as surprises? How do these little works get made?

A: In the beginning, I babbled happily: imaginary words, real feelings. Then I was taught; teachers clamped words like ice collars around the neck of my wild head. Real words, imaginary feelings. Now that I teach, I realize no one's listening. I head for my familiar wilderness and language flutters from the throat of my thoughts.

.
.
.

Into each life, a little brain must fall.

All good things come to those who bait.

The good stumble, the great fall.

You'll catch more flies with money.

People who live in salt houses shouldn't shed tears.

The good grumble, the great wail.

Better the anemone you know than the anemone you don't.

Abstinence makes the heart go wander.

The early worm gets eaten by the bird

MARTY RUBIN

Q: Some of your shorter pieces read like traditional proverbs, pieces of folk wisdom. Others are bitingly ironic. It's almost as if there's an angel over one of your shoulders and a devil over the other. How do you decide which to listen to? Or is it even your decision at all?

A: I just sit on the sidelines, bemused, and let the two of them fight it out. But I must confess, as I get older, the angel seems to be winning out.

⋮

Never underestimate the wisdom of being easily satisfied.

Some truths can only be seen in the dark.

No lily cares if it's the first.

The sea outlasts its storms.

Time does not pass, it continues.

Parrots mimic their owners. Their owners consider that a sign of intelligence.

Magic is not what magicians do, but what they can't do.

The pearl only weighs the oyster down.

Never hold an opinion longer than you can hold your breath.

Movement is the freedom of the body; stillness, of the mind.

Everything is real when it happens and a dream afterwards.

The difference between an ocean and a desert is Time.

Sometimes out of sheer perversity reality conforms to my wishes.

The pursuit of unhappiness always succeeds.

Life corrects the errors of logic.

Obedience corrupts; absolute obedience corrupts absolutely.

MIKE GINN

Q: You write comedy for TV, but your jokes/aphorisms also have a literary sensibility—for example, you sometimes allude to historic events. There used to be a bold line drawn between literature and pop culture. Is this line even relevant anymore?

A: That's a question of audience. Niche "content" seems to be the name of the game. Don't you love that word? Content? Say it. Content. *Content*. Con-tent. Mmmm. It makes me feel a little dead inside, just to hear it. In theory, now you can do just about anything. If you do it well enough, and an audience exists, they can find it. The bummer mandates of broad audience appeal are becoming less significant, I hope. If I'm living in my car when this book comes out, I'm going to look like a real idiot for saying that. But I feel hopeful. The divides in question are widening, and new voices seem to be filling the cracks.

⋮

Being 28 in 2016: I'm not ready for a relationship.
Being 28 in 1816: I have 13 kids.
Being 28 in 1000 BC: I lived a good life, thrice I ate a berry and once a pear.

2014: I'll make my life bad on purpose…for the comedy.
2017: I'm ready to live the good life…ironically.

Going to be taking some time offline to focus on the things that are important to—ok I'm back, let's do this.

Today an on-duty seeing eye dog growled at me.

It's that wonderful season where I call Target to ask if their world map shower curtains acknowledge Israel and get mad no matter what they say.

I hate it when I have exactly enough quarters to do laundry but then when I try to use the dryer I find one of them is a Canadian and I move to Canada to start a new life with only 25 cents to my name.

When everyone is screaming at you, that's how you know you had the best opinion.

Woman was singing along with "Crocodile Rock" at grocery store. When she noticed me looking at her she said, "I don't even like this song."

No sweeter feeling than finding out a TV show you already stopped watching is pissing everyone off.

Every time I watch Anthony Bourdain talk, I think, "Now there's a guy who definitely cheats on his wife."

Pardoning a turkey? The people you should be pardoning are incarcerated for nonviolent drug offenses. Keep the turkey pardon though, it's cute.

Just heard someone driving down the street honking their horn the whole time. Normally I'd be mad but tonight I think they made a good point.

If a friend is doing poorly be sure to make fun of them so they don't think that you think they're doing so bad they can't be made fun of.

I hate it when people complain a movie doesn't make sense. Look around you, dumbass, nothing makes sense.

My wife went back to school, left me for her mythology professor, and today my son referred to me as "the classic dunce archetype."

Guy 1: Who should be saying Don't Tread on Me?
Guy 2: How about a snake?
Guy 3: PERFECT! What could people trust more than a talking snake!?!

Started running whenever I get stressed, now I'm someplace in Chile and need a ride home.

Spent this morning's internal shower monologue ranting about how much better hexagonal pencils are than circle ones. Hope it comes up today!

"Don't put all your eggs in one basket" is a lie perpetuated by Big Basket to sell more baskets.

Women love to see the veins in a man's arm. It shows he runs on blood, and not something more sinister.

Watching Olympic ping pong and the guys' faces all have the same dull look that says, "It's too late for me to be this good at something else."

The oldest cat in the world just died at age 30 and the next oldest is 27. I'm 28 and I guess I'll always be older than every cat now.

Airbus is the worst brand name I've ever heard. "Hey, let's combine the airplane experience with the only worst travel available."

There's nothing more beautifully optimistic than a sign for a lost bird.

Can't wait to see how dudes figure out how to still get really mad at each other when cars are all self-driving.

JAMES GUIDA

Q: You write about "the mysterious disjunctions that can characterize the senses," or the "dim registers" of awareness. How does this affect your work, being a watcher who watches the world while also watching the watcher?

A: I love the side of the aphorism that's about observation of the mind and the senses at work, the sort of study of basic experience and what it can sometimes mean for our underlying conceptions. In the 18th century there's this explicit interest in "man"—(although an emphatic, often dubious division between the sexes was not uncommon) what he's supposed to consist of, how he may or may not be different from other animals and so forth. But a vein of species self-inquiry can be found in the work of aphorists in centuries before and after too. I like the idea of continuing that, and of trying to do so in light of things we know now. There's a kind of novelty and challenge interwound.

How the senses might appear in perfect concert in one setting but not in another, or the way one reigns seemingly to the exclusion of all else—a novelist might start by describing the phenomenon, then read a life or a story outward from it. For me the phenomenon itself is what's interesting: I want to know how it works, magnify it and sketch a picture, hunt for reverberations.

⋮

As with novels, romance seems to rarely endure without a strong beginning.

Ideally there would be two lives: one to live, the other for magazines.

No such thing, I've come to believe, as "just a pretty voice."

The amount of so-dubbed sharing going on now can make selfishness look like a virtue.

He can be kinder now that he has finally stopped trying to be so accommodating.

We say that so-and-so will end up alone, knowing full well that many who are worse don't. What's really meant perhaps is: "If he doesn't look out, he'll end up ...*himself.*"

All the same, people who strenuously don't want to be liked belong in the same category as those who do.

Another notion to be added to the magical category is that of "owning" something. While great in some applications, merely by saying "own it," any opinion or course of action at all can be totally transformed, celebrated and triumphantly adopted, though its wisdom was uncertain just a minute ago.

"I'm worried that doing such and such would make me a complete bastard."

"Just own it dude."

"Well alright then!"

The mysterious disjunctions that can characterize the senses at times—my hands still insist they can find what I need in a bag without actually looking inside it, never mind that they're confounded in this over and over again. Similarly, a friend says that when on the phone in her apartment, before hanging up she tends to walk to the front door, as though showing out the person on the other end of the line.

My view is that much liking and disliking occurs with little real connection to the object in question, and more from people's temperamental need to support or criticize or rage in general.

Half asleep in my ground-floor apartment in the morning, I sometimes hear the neighbors walking down the stairs and talking in the hall before leaving the building. For a moment I dimly register them as my family members, or then housemates from long ago.

Conundrum: it's only in not wanting anything from people that we can be halfway objective in our understanding of them, and yet, in that case, one of the things we don't want is to properly engage with them.

So much thought and feeling exists in, lives and hides in—the jaw.

He calls "opinionated" anyone who dares to be as particular as he is.

It has to be admitted that some are attractive on the inside, yet even then only under certain lighting.

C. likes to trash himself, and if you can implicitly be included in the onslaught too, all the better.

Defensiveness doesn't have nearly as bad a name as it deserves.

No matter how many times the genie had heard this particular first wish, he remained as surprised as before: that whenever a sparrow flies, the wisher could see the paths all somehow traced out and lingering in the air.

DENISE HAYES

Q: You have expressed a liking for writers like J.G. Ballard, Ray Bradbury, and Jorge Luis Borges, all known for writing either dark or fantastic work, or both. Whence comes your writerly interest in the shadow side?

A: I love the fantastic elements in these writers' stories—Borges' infinite and labyrinthine library, Ballard's crystallised jungle, Bradbury's hellish carousel—and the way each author explores the dark and surreal aspects of "what if?" scenarios. What if we could go on a time-travelling dinosaur safari? What if we never had to sleep? What if a world existed where lost objects were duplicated?

My interest in such speculative fiction was sparked by childhood comics such as *Creepy Worlds*, *Sinister Tales* and *Out of this World*. Such publications reflected the dawning of the space age in the late 1950s, and the growing centrality of Einsteinian physics. I was thrilled by glimpses of alien planets and captivated by the time-warping paradoxes invoked by faster-than-light-speed space flights. There was still plenty of "old world" superstition in these comics too and I was deliciously terrified by stories of haunted objects and uncanny encounters. Ballard describes the short story as a form "coined from precious metal, a glint of gold that will glow forever in the deep purse of your imagination," and these pocket-money purchases certainly formed an early repository of 'shadow-side' inspiration for my own writing.

⋮

We are so dazzled by the unicorn's golden horn we do not see the chains around her neck.

Woodpecker: black and white and red all over, hammering out the news. A red-top tabloid of the trees.

Puffin: a comical little concierge of the cliff face.

Winter trees: forked fractals of black lightning against snow-laden skies.

Masters of the universe? A simple sneeze reminds us we aren't even masters of our own nostrils.

Virtual Reality: not virtual, not real.

Serendipity do-dah, serendipity day. You never quite know what's coming your way.

OVERHEARD MALAPROPISMS

A PRESTIDITIOUS SCAPEGOAT

Whenever someone really gets my goat I go for the juggler.

SEND IN THE FROWNS

I tried to get back with my ex by tweeting him a jokey apology. Didn't work. Just a futile jester.

DO THE MATH

Teacher: What is meant by the word 'symmetry'?

Pupil 1: My gran was buried in one.

Pupil 2: I wonder if she found out everything was the same on the other side.

OVERHEARD (WHILE TRAVELLING)

I've always had to let my hair do what it wants.

If you're reading a book and have too many climaxes it can get boring.

WHAT A DIFFERENCE A DAY MAKES

Tonight I woke from a short sleep and thought the evening shadows were morning's dark deep. Then I heard the radio newsman mention it was Thursday night and my mind ran. If tomorrow is still today, yesterday's sad thoughts have now slipped softly away.

DEATH: AN EQUINE EPIPHANY

I remember, after she'd been given the tragic news, walking through the fields and saying to her, "Life is only one time. You will meet again." She just stared and laughed at a horse eating grass, with life tumescent between its legs, and said I had never been a friend.

BEAUTY: AN ORTHODONTIC EPIPHANY

On the bus-back journey today I heard two women talking about teeth. Then I saw how the sun was sinking, rippling turquoise skies with crimson light, and thought they could not miss the sight. Then one woman turned to look into the bright glowing redness of her friend's mouth.

SNAPSHOTS FROM LIFE

BABY

My baby plays an invisible harp, her fingers fluttering and plucking at the cavernous expanse of air above her.

LOVE'S OPIUM

Poppies were the lovers' favorite flower. They hardly dared breathe when their lips were close, for fear of petals falling.

DR. MARDY GROTHE

Q: Why do you think so many authors fail to realize their grand ambitions when they try their hand at aphorisms?

A: With apologies to Alvin Toffler, who wrote, "Parenthood remains the greatest single preserve of the amateur," I would argue that the great amateur art is the writing of aphorisms. For centuries, writers who would never—and who probably *should* never—write a novel have shown no hesitation when it came to the writing of aphorisms.

And why not? A novel is a huge undertaking, not unlike an attempt to scale Mount Everest. Only a small percentage of people ever attempt such a feat—and those who succeed in reaching the summit are greatly honored. But who among us can't *imagine* making the ascent, and maybe even walking awhile in the direction of the mountain? An aphorism may be seen as a baby step in the direction of immortality.

Over the last half century, I've taken thousands of such steps, and you will see twenty-seven of them in a moment. However, just as a person who's never climbed a mountain shouldn't say *I am a mountain climber*, I'm reluctant to look over my several thousand baby steps and say *I am an aphorist.* To do so takes far more chutzpah than I possess.

I am completely comfortable, though, in saying that I have penned more than 5,000 aphorisms in my lifetime. Most have appeared in "Dr. Mardy's Quotes of the Week," a free weekly e-newsletter I've been sending out to subscribers around the world for nearly two decades. *Short Circuits* represents the first time my creations have appeared in a published quotation anthology.

Most of the people reading this book are lovers of aphorisms, and every aphorism lover I've ever met has been occasionally moved to emulation (a tip of the hat here to Saul Bellow, who wrote, "A writer is a reader moved to emulation"). If this describes you, you might also agree with my assessment that composing aphorisms is a lot like throwing darts. For every bulls-eye, hundreds miss the mark (some by quite a bit), and countless others don't even hit the dartboard.

Q: How can writers, including you, ever know if their aphorisms are worthy?

A: With dart throwing, though, there is no self-deception, and almost all observers are in general agreement about the quality of any particular throw. However, with writers of aphorisms, self-deception is rampant, and it often happens that people think they've scored a bull's eye when they've completely missed the mark. This is true of writers of every genre, of course, and the phenomenon has shown up most famously in Sir Arthur Quiller-Couch's famous admonition, "Murder your darlings," which he offered to writers who believed they had "perpetrated a piece of exceptionally fine writing."

In my experience, however, the great mass of aphorism writers—and that includes me—almost never murder their darlings, and many are only too willing to parade them before the public. I've resolved that problem in this collection by taking myself out of the equation. I began by asking my most candid and constructive critic, my wife Katherine, to go over my entire collection and select what she regarded as 250 of the best (roughly five percent of the total). I then sent her selections to the editors, who chose what they regarded as the twenty-seven best for this publication. I hope you enjoy them.

⋮

Risk, someone once said, is one of life's sweeteners, and sweeteners, we now know, are one of life's risks.

It's one thing to yield to temptation after a struggle, but it's quite another to welcome it with a warm embrace.

In the battle between Good and Evil, Good is slightly disadvantaged because it plays by the rules.

Tact, *n.* Diplomacy in casual attire.

Reading is a way of achieving companionship without giving up solitude.

The answers to life's questions, like apparel, are not particularly elegant or attractive when selected from the one-size-fits-all rack.

Flattery, *n*. A crime that requires an accomplice.

Peace with others is impossible when you're at war with yourself.

Speed-reading may be impressive, but it is about as satisfying as speed-eating.

What we fail to mention in our descriptions of ourselves is almost always more important than what we actually say.

Nostalgia, *n*. Life in the past lane.

Taking things and people for granted is the most common form of ingratitude.

Maturity is when you accept that the person you've become is not necessarily the person you wanted to be.

Here's a rule of thumb that might serve you well: if you have a great mind, work on your heart; if you have a great heart, work on your mind.

People who say "I understand exactly how you feel" never understand exactly how you feel.

If you don't love your work, it's hard to love your life.

If you are offended by bad odors, don't rummage around in the trash.

A problem denied is worse than a problem exaggerated.

Some things emerge from places so deep inside us that they appear to come from the outside.

People reveal far more about themselves when describing other people than they do when describing themselves.

Never rely on your friends for money, or on your money for friends.

The worst memory may be the one that remembers too much.

We don't see things the way they are, we are because of the way we see things.

When writing becomes difficult, try speaking the words; when speaking becomes difficult, try writing them down.

When gazing into a mirror, beauty looks for signs of ugliness, and ugliness for signs of beauty.

The heart is able to fool the head far more often than the head is able to fool the heart.

Ascetic, *n.* A person who takes the minimum to the maximum.

OLIVIA DRESHER

Q: I think of the work you share on Twitter and want to ask you what your process is when you move the material from online to print form.

A: All of my writings in this anthology came from Twitter. When I gathered together the fragments and aphorisms, they were recent material (most of them date back to early 2016). I began posting my fragments at Twitter in Fall 2009, so I had over 55,000 to choose from. I write everything there spontaneously, and only edit when I'm gathering together fragments to be published, though I edit very little (sometimes I add line breaks). Hence the tweets were spontaneously written and spontaneously chosen. Spontaneity, for me, is one aspect of fragmentary writing. I want to capture consciousness as it's lived, in the moment.

Q: By founding and editing *FragLit*, your online international "magazine of fragmentary writing," you were instrumental in publishing and publicizing forms that might not otherwise

have had a venue. What is it about fragmentary forms that you find either attractive or pertinent to early 21st century writing?

A: Our lives are fragmented in the early 21st century, and our writings reflect our lives. I'm drawn to writing that doesn't have a plot, writing that is outside of a traditional genre. I'd say that what I find to be most attractive about fragmentary writing is the way it's broken up, and its brevity. For with brevity there's a sense of immediacy, and that's what draws people to the writing. I love the challenge of shaping perceptions into as few words as possible.

⋮

It begins with the weather
and how much sleep you've had
the night before.

Curiosity: part ego, part humility.

When you don't try, you are diminished.
When you try too hard,
you are a caricature of yourself.

The palm trees in L.A. have no soul.
It's just Hollywood gossip
when they sway in the breeze.

I turn to humor
when seriousness doesn't work.
I turn to seriousness
when humor doesn't work.

When nothing is quite the way it is…
and yet it seems to be.

One perfect night of closeness
isn't something to remember,
it's something to remind you
of all the imperfect nights to come.

Sorrow is a frozen bell.

When language isn't a bridge,
it's a weapon.

Morning isn't trying to wipe out night.
They're just taking turns.
It's a conversation.

My writing comes from that place
that wants to set me free.

Every loss I experience tries to remind me
that the final loss is coming.

Who you are
when you can't escape
from who you are,
that's who you are.

No moods, just consciousness.

Feelings want to be free;
Thoughts want to be right.

Billions of people …
and not one of them is you.

If you can share hopelessness,
there's hope.

An attraction is a warning sign.

In the grocery store:
Ten avocados for $10.
Outside, a homeless man yelling.

What do crows think of hummingbirds.

1962, he said.
Immediately I thought of that year:
the Cuban missile crisis,
being let out of school.
But he meant $19.62.
I gave him a $20.

Humans will eat anything
and believe anything.

A few narrow pathways in the forest
and a thousand longings.

How blatantly people hide these days.

I was feeling peaceful,
sitting on a bench in the sun…
until a stranger walked by and said,
"Don't look so sad, smile!"

When the flesh asks the skeleton to dance.

Truth cleans the wound with no anesthetic.

Everything is on its way to leaving.
Everything and everyone.

The way nature never holds back
but humans almost always do.

JAMES LOUGH

Q: You teach a course called The Art of the Sentence. Why break it down so small?

A: I'm interested in sentences as lines, or channels, of energy and meaning. Readers suffer through books full of flat prose, the words dead on the page. But there's also prose that leaps off the page, vibrating with energy. Dead writing and vibrant writing both feature black words on white pages, so the energy has to be a function of the writing and the writer.

Add a visual image to a sentence and you amp up its energy via emotional power. Throw in a profound topic, and the strong current can electrify a reader. Emily Dickinson wrote, "If I feel physically as if the top of my head were taken off, I know that is poetry." Electric sentences come more easily to a writer whose own energy is strong and whose attention is self-aware—a writer open to a *felt* sense of life. Hindu poetics uses a word: *rasa*. It means the poet's emotional energy (flavor) while writing the poem. The energy enters the poem and is preserved there, as in a battery. When a reader in an open state encounters the poem, the poem's energy then enters the reader.

And the aphorism is a perfect form for experimenting with lexical energies—one sentence at a time.

⋮

My religion is Aphorism. My God is a short and witty God.

Some of us are guarded by shields so intricate and interesting we forget they're shields, barriers, force fields of fear.

Obviously, nobody's better than anyone else. But some people are clearly worse.

I looked in the bathroom mirror this morning and thought, "It's still me."

"Buck up" really means push it down and pass it on to your children.

What they don't know won't hurt them, but it might hurt us.

URGENT: We have determined the journey is more important than the goal.
SOLUTION: Effective immediately, the journey is our new goal.

Words are particular about which word sits down next to them in a sentence—they know a word is judged by the company it keeps.

We're all addicted to something—booze, drugs, screens, sex, food, caffeine. And if not these, we're addicted to self-righteousness.

A shrewd way to mask an addiction is to become an enthusiast, a connoisseur of what you're addicted to.

If revenge is sweet *and* a dish best served cold, then the best revenge is ice cream.

Doing heroin will lead you to smoke marijuana, which opens the door to beer, then you'll try pretzels and peanuts, and before long you'll find yourself eating vegetables.

Philo-sopher = lover of wisdom
Philo-philer = lover of love
Fala-faler = lover of deep fried garbanzo balls

Life is short, and time flies when you're having fun, so have as little fun as possible.

If you're an only child, you learn self-reliance; one of two children, you learn competition; one of three: politics.

Wine glasses must wait for a toast to become reacquainted.

In hammering all idols, we idolize the hammer.

Feelings of superiority are well grounded…in feelings of inferiority.

It must be exhausting always having to be oneself.

Cynicism: despair with a diploma.

Profound raptures usually follow profound ruptures.

"No dogma" is itself a dogma, "No rules," is a rule, and "No limits" limits limits.

Less is more, more or less.

When we reread a book, we trade larger surprises for smaller ones.

When searching for the truth, a good place to start is among the smoking ruins.

Curious, how the verb "to weather" forks into two opposite meanings: "to erode" and "to endure." And reveals our most basic challenge.

As I grow older, I am humbled by the lasting power of my flaws.

What's amazing is that we can sit back and watch our thoughts carrying on as if they didn't come from us. Possibly they didn't.

Maybe we have in fact discovered a perpetual motion machine, and it is life itself.

Stars, pinpricks in a black sky, as if tearing the fabric of the night would uncover nothing but light.

We sleep, our bodies curved like question marks, as if only when unconscious do we admit we have no answers.

Maybe we die when we have finally accumulated more memories than our minds can hold, and dementia is an attempt to cheat the process.

In one way or another, we are all broken people. There is a great relief in this.

LANCE LARSEN

Q: Your aphorisms are among the shortest in the book, and they almost always feature imagery. Can you "talk" about verbal efficiency and visual imagery?

A: When it comes to reading aphorisms I'm drawn to whatever shakes up my literary landscape. When it comes to writing them, I default to concreteness. Blame my training in poetry and Ezra Pound's nagging voice defining the image: "that which presents an intellectual and emotional complex in an instant of time." Imagery provides a kind of aura to whatever is said outright, which allows the language to pulse and squiggle a little.

Q: What's the difference then between a short poem and an aphorism?

A: Poems have secret zippers; aphorisms snap up the front. Poems are Mistress Bradstreet; aphorisms are that long-haired tinkerer, Benjamin Franklin. Poems are Havarti or Brie; aphorisms have a cheese-like taste but a more mordant crunch. Poems sashay into a room then disappear around the corner, all perfume; aphorisms clump through the front door and stand in the hall, big handed and wise, ready to declaim. How can anyone choose between them?

Q: So what exactly do you get when you try to cross them?

A: I don't know, but be prepared to disappoint the in-laws.

$$\vdots$$

Great journeys begin not with a first step but a door left ajar.

To climb a new mountain, wear old shoes.

Theory is a leaky cup.

We fill the hummingbird feeder not out of charity but to attract some rubied quickness we know we lack.

Look at that celebrity soar!—like a worm in the beak of a hungry bird.

Wonder is the yeast of the imagination.

Fraud or Freud: for seven drafts not even my spell check could tell the difference.

Envy the young their ignorance, not their perfect bodies.

What begins in glances flowers in groins.

Junk drawers have a gorgeously tangled order. So too long marriages.

The older I get the higher I rise—on the Grim Reaper's to-do list.

Rather than jump to conclusions, crawl towards them, as if through broken glass, letting the evidence cut you along the way.

Gesundheit!—as close as I've come to Nietzsche and Heidegger in months.

One doesn't read Paul Celan so much as consent to be interviewed by darkness.

The savvy have mastered the art of passing off their passions as stumbles, like the prep boy on the crowded bus who just happens to bump against the girl he loves. Or like me at the Guggenheim in Bilbao, ricocheting my way through Richard Serra's spiraling iron walls, disguising my greedy touches as clumsiness.

Even Rembrandt tried to avoid painting hands.

Water knows the low spots better than a bevy of engineers.

The beginning ventriloquist talks in his sleep, the seasoned ventriloquist in everyone else's.

Men are broken toys. Some look to the sky and whisper, Mend me, mend me. Others cry, Break me again.

Promises made under duress are spinier than sea urchins.

Shame is measured not as the crow flies, but as the gopher burrows.

The thief knows better than the homeowner which hinges need oiling.

ISAAC FELLOWS

Q: Can you give me some insight into your creative process, specifically in regard to the pieces that have been selected for this anthology?

A: IN THE MIND GARDEN THERE ARE SEVERAL VOICES

1. What can I say about this?

2. Don't you mean these?

3. I can say that these are the worst of them.

4. The worst?

5. The best are those that were never written. The ones I caught naked while walking. The wild ones still in their wilderness.

6. Second best are those the editors rejected.

7. Semi-domesticated?

8. Never fully broken-in.

9. And these are the worst?

10. Say third-best. The ones that live in houses now.

11. Think of them never being read.

12. Never being read!

13. Still wild in the minds of the readers who will never read them.

14. And what about the readers who will?

15. Hello.

⋮

I'm so sad, says a crow. A demon notices and offers the crow some solace. Oh that's okay, says the crow, I don't want any solace. But your sadness, says the demon, your sadness is so oppressive. Let me take that weight from you. Oh that's okay, says the crow. I wasn't sad. I was only pretending. You do know that there's no end to pretending for crows. You do know, says the demon, that there's no end to solace. Everything ends, says the crow. The demon shakes its head. Only pretending.

A mole has gotten to the bottom of things when he finds the bones of a dog. The dog bones shiver and whisper. The mole strains to hear. What was that, the mole asks. The dog bones hold very still and whisper very softly. The mole can hear them now. Is that so, asks the mole. I would never have thought. The mole leaves the bones be and returns to the surface. He goes to write down what the dog bones said but the words keep slipping from him. Maybe there aren't any words, says a demon. The demon plays a tune on a bone flute. The mole heads back underground.

A woman carves her likeness into a log and tips it into the river. There goes, she says. By the time she makes it to the ocean she is old and bent and full of worry, not about the likeness but the secret chamber she'd carved out of the log, the place where she'd hidden a small glass heart. What will have become of that, she wonders. As she walks along the beach a demon joins her. There are so many logs tumbled about. Hers could be any of them. You can simulate all you like, says the demon. But you'd do better reading books made of air. The woman winces. She's cut her foot on something.

A demon considers dancing on the head of a pin but can't remember the origin of that reference so puts it off. Anyway, it might hurt, she says. But she can't stop thinking about it. And thinking for demons is above being, so before long there's this whopping great pin rising before her into space. I could dance on that, she thinks. And just like that she's up in space on the head of the pin spinning with her arms upraised. But then she notices all the others. Who invited them, she wonders. I'm out. And just like that she's back on earth riding some poor soul's shoulders. Let them do the dancing, she thinks.

A demon tells a man that he's got to stop kidding himself. And then I'll be happy, supposes the man. The demon doesn't say anything. If I stop kidding myself, says the man, then I'll be happy. He looks to the demon. But the demon's mum. Who am I kidding, says the man, I don't know the first thing about any of this. Yourself, says the demon. Myself what, asks the man. Knock knock, says the demon. Who's there, asks the man. Yourself, says the demon. Yourself who, asks the man. Your cell awaits, says the demon. One step ahead of you, says the man.

From the crow's point of view the garbage pit is a fine place to spend an afternoon. Nothing better, he thinks, than picking through all this crap. Then a demon appears beside him and asks, But crow, wouldn't you rather have an expense account? It takes only a moment to get you registered. Only a moment, wonders the crow. Hotels, says the demon. Air travel. Restaurants. The crow considers. There was this deep-fried thing he got once from a dumpster behind a restaurant. It was so good. But what's this, says the crow, tossing aside small green bags of dog waste. A plastic silver ring!

A fly lands in the mouth of a corpse. This'll do, she says. There's a spot beside a gold-crowned molar where the light's especially good. She sits there and reads. It's taken her several lifetimes but she knows that eventually she'll finish Pride and Prejudice. And the thing is, it just keeps getting better.

A chickadee lands on a sunflower and closes his eyes. I've had enough, he thinks. This is the end. A demon sits on the chickadee's wing. You don't know that, says the demon. Yes I do, protests the chickadee. No, actually, you don't, says the demon. Think about it. The chickadee thinks about the end. But he finds he can't fix his mind on whatever it is that the end means. I know what the end means, he says, trying to convince himself. The sun comes out. Its rays pass through the demon becoming a rainbow across the chickadee's wing. Well isn't that pretty, he says. And it is.

WILLIAM PANNAPACKER
(WERNER TWERTZOG)

Q: How do you think wearing a mask, in this case the persona of filmmaker Werner Herzog, changes what you write? In these aphorisms, is it possible to determine where "Herzog" ends and "Pannapacker" begins?

A: As Twertzog would say, "The self is but a mask." I write the tweets; the topics come from my daily stream of consciousness, but they are shaped by an ongoing engagement with the director's style and intellectual preoccupations as expressed in his films and interviews.

"Twertzog" is based on Werner Herzog, but he is not limited by him. Twertzog tweets things that Herzog might not say but that Twitter followers would be pleased if he had said, in his famous Bavarian accent.

Would it not be fascinating if the great director had a phobia of yogurt? Or if he held ripped-from-the-headlines positions on U.S. politics? Or if he had a bantering relationship with the Slovenian provocateur Slavoj Žižek? Twertzog fills a need for public commentary—in an admiringly satirical style—from a widely revered figure who has better things to do with his time.

⋮

Fish grew legs to escape the horrors of the deep.
And whales lost legs to escape the horrors of the land.

Giraffes do not have long necks
Merely for eating leaves
But because they yearn
To escape the earth
And voyage to the stars.

I can no longer tell the difference between the beards of hipsters, the orthodox, the homeless, the simply mad, and the English professors.

Please place your emotional baggage in the overhead bins, unless it is too large, in which case you can unload it on your fellow passengers.

Zoos, as we all know, are important for making humans think they are free because they do not live in literal cages.

Love is patient. Love is kind. Love is the leading cause of murder.

Americans walk on eggshells in public to save up murderous rage for the Internet.

I would like an emoji that expresses the fleeting state of consciousness between terror and the sublime.

The reason we are told to "think outside the box" in business is to grant permission to ignore all ordinary rules of prudence and decency.

When a tree falls in the forest, it does, of course, make a sound, because, you need to realize, it is not all about you.

The day on which you start thinking about your "personal brand" is the day on which you begin to no longer be an actual person.

You must remember this about the old: They have lost an entire world and probably everyone who loved them when they were young.

In America, athletic events must begin with coercive nationalism. Because freedom.

Americans: You do not need standing desks. You need treadmills that hurl you into open graves the moment you stop working.

The young should get more votes than the old, since the young are forced to deal with the long-term consequences of elections.

In America, it is important to "do what you love," because then you will work for lower wages.

It's important
To tell the young
They can be "Anything they can dream,"
So that, one day,
They'll blame themselves,
Instead of the system.

I am told death is the new forty.

Stop repeating, "To be honest." It causes me to assume you normally are a liar.

Sorry, my child, self-actualization is for the rich. We must content ourselves with high-fructose corn syrup.

KARL KEMPTON

Q: Can you briefly explain what visual poetry means to you and why you find it an attractive or useful form of expression?

A: Our culture has lost much of its visual language play and art caused by the printing press requirements of the x-y grid for reading and economies of business scale habits. The modern art period gave birth to a new visual text art, most of which has been ignored except the calligramme. After WW2 visual text art, such as the highly advanced painted word, earned a wide following elsewhere.

I began my visual poetry with the typewriter in 1973 restricting myself to the x-y weaver-grid composing a work one line at a time. Composing with computer has allowed greater freedom, a wider field in which to compose.

Q: In some of your works, the denotative meanings of the words are crucial; in others, they seem to serve only as design elements. Is this an accurate reading? How do you decide which route to take?

A: My dyslexic brain "wiring" energizes letter-gymnastics within words. Sometimes letters disappear. I have been given the gift to see poems inside words. Over the years I developed a keen sense for new visual possibilities studying visual text and iconographic arts from rock art to contemporary visual poetry and word painting.

Lexical or visual poems arrive in a visual flash. I look upon myself as an intuitive stenographer in waiting. I do not seek a poem unless an incomplete series has been triggered or on the hunt for the found poem.

⋮

the epic of now

O

the hourglass throat

w   b

(((om)))

t   m

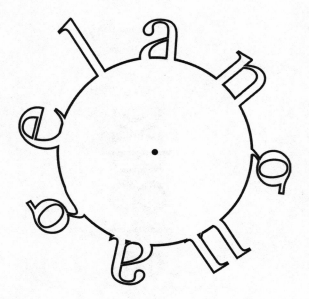

missing the point

(lesson)

1.

mindless x ( ) = less mind

2.

nowhere x ( ) = now here

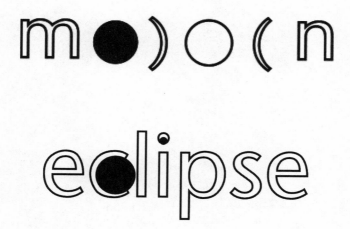

CHARLENE DEGUZMAN

Q: In your work, you manage to walk a fine line between light-heartedness and morbid humor -- sometimes, like a song with a happy melody and sad lyrics, the tone contrasts with the message. How do you manage to balance the two? Or do you have a choice at all?

A: I actually never see it as two separate things. For me, it isn't about trying to balance anything—it's just about being honest, about being myself. Whenever I tweet something, I'm just sharing an actual thought, idea, or experience I had. Maybe the humor is what my brain uses to survive. If it weren't funny, I'd probably be dead.

.
.
.

I love when I tweet something and someone immediately texts me to check in.

Wow bowling is kinda therapeutic when you visualize yourself as the ball and the pins are the debilitating horror of the state of the world.

Shhh. Go to sleep. Everything you're worried about will still be there tomorrow.

He loves me He loves me not He loves me. Kicked out of this flower shop again.

Parties are just a bunch of people in their 20s posing for a photo that nobody is taking.

I can't wait to get married and discuss the farmer's market from two different rooms over the sound of clipping toeneails.

You could die today. Have fun!

Ate alone at a counter but sat next to a guy also eating alone. Ordered, ate, paid, and left at the exact same time. I think I'm dating!

Instead of making fake plans let's genuinely say goodbye.

Sorry I'm late, I didn't wanna come.

Girl if you're reading his horoscope before yours, you gotta love yourself harder.

Whenever I hear sirens I like to imagine the driver just realized he is in love.

I can't believe you didn't invite me. I mean I wouldn't have gone, but still.

Your ex is posting passive-aggressive gym pics again.

I am so humiliated by my younger self. Wait, am I humiliating my future self …right …now? (Doesn't move for 20 minutes)

My social event vibe could best be described as "Girl Who Can Watch Your Stuff."

FASHION TIP: your coping mechanisms are showing.

Girl likes boy. Boy doesn't like girl. Girl runs off with other boy. Girl is trapped in a cult. I need you to pick me up in Allentown, PA.

Kinda weird that we're all out there trying to pair off despite the fact that all people are absolutely terrifying.

Please don't let all of my good news fool you I am still putting gas in my '97 Toyota Corolla 7 bucks at a time.

PAUL PORTUGÉS

Q: Why the short form?

A: Nothing more to say.

⋮

when

a   It's

child   something   in

dies   you   you

                    keep   like

                                        a

                                        bomb

without

you   bear

how   the   on

could   wild   the

I   grasses   unkempt

                                        graves

making

love   he

to   kisses   as

make   her   if

babies   eyes   God

                               were

                               inside

                               her

pressed   from

violets   my   as

fall   daybook   I

                               write

                               about

                               her

bullets

curse   who

barrio   eat   then

poets   them   spit

             like   out

             dulces   histories

                          of

                          pain

JOHN BRADLEY

Q: Some of your aphorisms perform an instant swing from the infinitesimal to the infinite almost like a camera lens honing in on a tiny detail and then suddenly zooming out again to show the big picture. This reminds me of some theories of the sublime in art. Are you consciously applying these principles or it just a coincidence?

A: "O God, I could be bound in a nutshell, and count myself a king of infinite space," Hamlet tells us in a statement that sounds a lot like an aphorism. There's something almost miraculous about how the bit of prose we call the aphorism can contain both the minuscule and the immense. I'm not familiar with theories of the sublime in art, so I'm not consciously trying to achieve sublimity (though I always enjoy the stay).

I am, however, trying to create a sense of movement. I think all aphorisms, if memorable, achieve some sort of velocity. Writers find different ways to do this, but most provide a twist by the aphorism's closing. For example, Sarah Manguso writes, in her *300 Arguments*: "Worry is impatience for the next horror." She begins by defining an abstraction with another abstraction: "Worry is impatience...." It's interesting, but it produces no frisson. Manguso's last five words, however, create velocity: "...waiting for the next horror."

But I also hope the aphorism might reveal something about this world: The mouse droppings stuck to the bottom of the milk carton track back to the Milky Way.

$$\vdots$$

We chart our path like a dung beetle, rolling the future by the light of the Milky Way.

How is it that Einstein's brain weighs the same as my rubber boot?

That rash on my wrist—a great civilization once thrived there.

Blood wears many masks, but rarely its own.

I'd really like to be honest with you, but that's one of the Seven Deadly Virtues.

Had you arrived sooner, I could now be relaxing somewhere in the future.

A burial should always take place where a burial has never taken place.

Live like bread—rise up against yourself.

I once had the honor of picking up the dry cleaning of a famous poet. When I brought it to her office she glared at me and said, *This better not end up in one of your poems.*

Those infected with fame know only one cure—more fame.

Missing from the acknowledgements: *Written while under the influence of America.*

How to live a fruitful life: Avoid all tips on how to live your life.

TOM FARBER

Q: After decades of writing fiction and creative nonfiction, why did you immerse yourself in 'the epigrammatic'?

A: After the windy prose of my literary youth, I unconsciously moved toward concision and the episodic. Word-music and structured brevity of the partial, I intuited, could say more than enough. Decades of such books of prose foreshadowed the explicitly epigrammatic, which for me began in middle age. Suddenly, narrative insinuated unwarranted coherence. Taking stock of human folly, not to mention mayhems of our (too?)-successful species, with epigrams I could illuminate foible/self-deception/sentimentality. Disenchanted, hooked on working toward verbal prime numbers, dispensing with story in pursuit of irreducible conclusion, a skeptic or spoilsport might have...the last word.

Q: But then why, in each of your books of 'the epigrammatic,' do you include a companion essay?

A: Though for the last twenty years epigrams have been a kind of default setting, I've never renounced narrative. Yet one more novel, two memoirs, a screenplay. (My) epigrams are a wicked pleasure: hyperbolic, promising more than they can deliver. The essays function as counterpoint. It seems the better part of me has had to justify and debunk obsession with such a miraculously inveigling form.

⋮

"You wasted your life," she says, flattering herself and him.

"Don't speak ill of the dead."
Next thing you know, they'll be telling us not to speak ill of the living!

Q: "Have I wasted my whole life?"
A. "No. Not yet."

Spring: making light of winter's sorrows.

"Pornography is rape"—1980s argument with a certain thrust to it. Hyperbole as verbal violence, forcing submission to the arguers' (rapacious) fantasy of dominating the private lives of others.

When painter Mark Rothko said "Silence is so accurate," silence is what he broke.

Memoirist on book tour, yet again retelling the story of the story of her life.

Domestication: to breed in captivity.
Dogs, ducks.
Silk-moths, cows.
Llamas, goldfish.
Husbands, wives.

Second childhood: when you get to change your own diaper.

In the agnostic's afterlife, you may or may not get free of your own worst enemy.

Writer: someone who can't go without saying.

KEVIN GRIFFITH

Q: Death, old age, or even the period that ends a sentence. Whence comes your interest in endings?

A: The only certainty in life is that things will end. But it is such a nagging certainty, right? Why can't we be certain that we will be loved, or be happy, or find peace? Only endings loom before us. So my little works are ways of confronting that certainty and controlling it a bit. They are like nervous chuckles, those tiny laughs we all resort to when dealing with something oh so awful but oh so inevitable. Keep in mind, though, that if all good things come to an end, all bad things do too.

⋮

Life, Death, Meaning. Three things not included on my so-called everything bagel.

Old age: The nightmare we planted as a child that slowly grows into who we are.

When the dead speak, I can see my lips moving.

Death: Always voted most likely to succeed.

When the umbrella is broken, the wind cannot harm it anymore.

Why would I lie in the bed I had just made?

It's never too late to get an early start.

Never always describes itself in one word.

You cannot use light to see the light.

Even a bottomless pit has a top.

How long ago was before time began?

If a black hole swallows itself, what does it become?

No matter how many birds you use, you cannot kill even one stone.

The life you want is always longer than the one you have.

The period: The black hole that ends every thought.

Eternity is always open.

Death always has room for one more.

The same iceberg that sank the ship didn't stand a chance against global warming.

There's no place like nowhere.

The river's answer to everything is more river.

KU

A Ku is an exquisitely compressed form of the haiku. Like the haiku it consists of three lines, but instead of the traditional 5/7/5 syllable pattern, the lines have 5/7/5 *letter* limit.

Failed Messiah

Walks
through
water

The Giant's Problem

Birds
fly into
yawns

An Atheist Prays

Nails
words to
doubt

No One's Problem

Dying
too many
times

Stay in Your Homes

Whale
dreaming
wings

Faith

No man
unprays
a hope

Unbearable Silence

Tiger
nearing
a baby

STEVEN CARTER

Q: When did your aphorism writing sensibilities begin to take shape and how have they progressed?

A: When I started writing aphorisms, like so many lucky souls I happened on James Geary, who opened a number of doors for me. In no particular order of chronology or merit, these included: E. M. Cioran, Karl Kraus, Marie von Eschenbach, Goethe, La Rouchefoucauld, Kafka, Mark Twain, James Richardson, Don Paterson and Geary himself, who got his own start substituting aphorisms for fortunes in a Chinese fortune cookie factory.

Geary, and the voices speaking through him, showed me that aphorisms are a form of poetry (and vice versa). This seems to me important for several reasons, but since I must be brief let me say that, rather than function as verbal algorithms, good aphorisms usually feature a touch of ambiguity. Unlike poetry, however, they may contain the seeds of opposite ways of looking at the same thing.

Geary and others emphasize the importance of process in writing aphorisms. An aphorism is never finished as long as it keeps resonating in the reader's mind. As for the aphorist him/herself, a healthy respect for the muses is always a good thing. To invoke the latter-day muse of Keats, an aphorism must unfold "as naturally as leaves to a tree." The old clunker, "Time is an illusion," makes imperfect sense. Death herself = the perfect illusion.

⋮

Children don't feel minor or petty anguish. Children feel anguish.

Be driven to your knees. Let no one help you up—save someone who doesn't love you.

Only the unimaginable is real.

Scratch an itch with a foreign object—a Chinese backscratcher, a long-handled shower brush—and the relief is always different, "purer," than if you did so with your own fingers. And yet it is, was, the same itch.

TV sitcoms are the perfect allegory of life. Essentially all that happens is that people come in and go out of doors.

"We are no more related to our past selves than we are our future selves."— And our present selves? —*Especially our present selves.*

O the felicitous phrase—*enigmatic clarity*: it too is a glass key to "meaning."

Alienation: the crippling conviction that one is a minority of one.

Faith and hope: mortal enemies.

The traditional novel is dead. So what? So is the traditional reader.

In Paradise there was no verb but to be.

BRIAN JAY STANLEY

Q: You write both mini-essays and one-line aphorisms. What do you see as the appeal or advantages of either or both?

A: Some of the selections here are condensations of my long-form aphorisms/mini-essays; I've also expanded or incorporated mini-essays into full essays. I'm intrigued by how an idea works differently depending on how fully you develop it.

Some ideas prefer a long or short form over the other. There are complex thoughts that become merely cryptic when you over-tighten them; there are pregnant thoughts that become flaccid when you expand them. More often, I find ideas to be interesting—and interestingly different—at multiple levels of detail. In the short form, the thought may be suggestive and inconclusive and full of possibility. More fully developed, the thought leaves less to interpretation but satisfyingly maps out some of the richness of the world. This doesn't just apply to aphorisms. Articles get expanded into books, lyric and epic poetry can cover the same themes, but because the length of the form affects what the content reveals, you can read them all without a feeling of redundancy.

Idealism begins as the love of what ought to be, ends as the hatred of what is.

An epiphany is a whim that sticks.

We perish of boredom in the country and of fury in the city.

Depressed minds are like airplanes: they must keep moving in order not to crash.

Drunks taste their liquor least.

In foreign countries I experience life like a deaf person, interpreting faces instead of phrases.

Traveling abroad makes home a foreign land when I return.

A common enemy makes former enemies friends.

Celebrities enjoy every luxury except privacy. Fame grants them access to privileged places but bars them from common places.

The Victorian bachelor, bursting with decades of pent passion, fought the daily inner war of being a gentleman with genitals.

At holidays we make donations to the economy in each other's honor.

Happiness is the pursuit of nothing.

The blind hear best, the deaf see best. Like wind through a narrow pass, the world enters us more forcefully when it must squeeze through a single sense.

Our ancestors discovered wildernesses, we designate wildernesses. They built fences to protect civilization from the wild; we, to protect the wild from civilization.

Obstetricians keep undertakers in business.

The young have health and leisure but no money. The middle-aged have health and money but no leisure. The old have money and leisure but no health.

Death transforms the body from earth's most precious to its most repulsive substance.

Individuals create world history as drops of water bursting inaudibly on pavement create the rhythmic sound of rain.

BHANU KAPIL

1. WHAT IS THE SHAPE OF YOUR BODY?

Sometimes in the spaces, there is fear. Choose one:
1. The body of a woman, how she moves through the day.
2. Inside her: lolling oblongs, a little runny.
3. As seen through the mosquito net.
4. The translucencies of Sigmar Polke.
5. I don't know anything.

Artificial resin, lacquer on synthetic fabric. Substances that caused the surface to change colour. Silver oxide, red lead, cobalt chloride. Lanterns. Transparent polyester. Layered washes of lacquered colours and resins.

I don't know where to begin. But I know

my elbow, my back tooth: throbbing

I must.

1. HOW SHE MOVES

"I keep looking over my left shoulder, to see if he's still there."

My name, my body. Such versions, I occupy. Live in, as surely as a dung-wall house, a house that does not turn, is not born twice: skulls, oranges. A ladder leaning against a eucalyptus tree. A black hen with her red beak, in a basket of straw in the tree next to the front door of the house. Where I live. With a man whose one-eyebrow joins together. (Blown ash.) Plum blossoms. Mango orchard. Rooster. Two eggs; bees. A very dark brown horse. A clay oven. Honey. The sun. A cinnamon Liqueur, he brings me. I gulp then sleep, stunned by the sweetness of nouns. He has made altars of peacock feathers, *paise*, tiny mirrors, a dried stem of jasmine that is taller than I am. Then I'm awake. Wild salt of his chest and belly. A bed.

It may be that I have taken an irreversible action. (Woody smoke.)
A goat skin drying on the clothes line.

2. HER BODY

I risk lemons. I risk melted honey. I risk water. I risk an old wine bottle that has the shape of a Dravidian goddess. Her abandoned torso. Her hips. The massive sloping stubs of her transparent shoulders: I risk. The green glass of this body walking, slowly, along the orchard path. Balancing the lemon-ade on my head.

3. HER EYES

It is difficult today. The orchard. (Making something.) I see making a shape there. Dragging a black tarp under the farthest mango tree, over the old skins and nettles. I began to. But stopped.

4. HER SURFACE

Red clay. A dry river-bed. I'm scared of the dogs. I'm scared of the cow-men. No. I'm not from here. My hair loosely braided, oily, not kempt. My body gets smokey. Gets holes in it; its layers of bright cotton. No. I was, without a doubt, born in an English-speaking country. A country I could no longer tolerate.

5. WHAT SHE KNOWS

Shame may be fatal. I am here now. How I got here: gravity. The long dark of the border of Pakistan and India. Speed faster than color. Not being a man, I bleed like this. To arrive seasonal, in pain, not what he thought.

I am not beautiful. I couldn't even look into the faces of the air hostesses. Only the darkness around them. At a slant.

Salt. Rose. The colour black between the stars, beneath tongues. The darkness of our bedroom when we blow out the candles. The coals and the ash in the *ingiti* at dusk. The sound of a man working with nails and a hammer, as I write this. Later after *chai*, we'll have our bath. Salt crystals from Goa. Rose-water from an Indian grocery stop in the East End of London. It is difficult. He is always with me. These are the scraps.

2. WHO ARE YOU AND WHOM DO YOU LOVE?

A month from now. A week from now. Tomorrow. When he goes. The going. I'll make crepes, walk by the river with the dog, float candles in a pudding basin; the usual. He's gone. Between our bodies: the sun at 5 a.m.; fifty-seven Herefords, and a Brahma bull that broke the river fence; four and a half thousand hummingbirds; a dying man; a man who is about to knock on the door of a woman with black eyes, to tell her that he loves her; the woman herself, who is drawing a bath. She can't hear the door above the water. And her eyes aren't really black. They're brown. She lights a match.

Floating candles. The incommensurable distance. I forgot to memorize his face.

3. DESCRIBE A MORNING YOU WOKE WITHOUT FEAR

The Ganges at Hardwar. Dusk. Steps. For two rupees, I buy a boat of palm leaves. It holds a diva: tiny earthenware pot, oil, a wick. I light a match. Push the boat into the river with my hands. Years later, the Pacific foam boiling at my feet, invisible whales migrating north, like the stars at daybreak, I try to remember that night. That version of water. I can't.

I remember the oiliness of my fingertips, and the smell of human flesh, upriver, burning. Frothy crusts, steam: the smell, also, of hot milk being poured, brass bowl to brass bowl, *dudh*, thick syllable, at the top of the steps. How I sat for hours, drinking the hot, sweet, milky tea, my last night there before I headed south, to Jaipur. A red desert. The opposite of a sea. Its aftermath.

4. WHERE DID YOU COME FROM / HOW DID YOU ARRIVE?

"May I?"

"If you'd like."

"What are you writing about?"

"Nothing."

"I've been watching you."

"What do I look like, then?"

"I don't know. Your hair keeps falling over your face. Are you Muslim or something?"

"No. Zoroaster."

"Zarathustra?"

"I'm not a member of a cult."

And then, the names I'd never heard before: Brecht, Eno, Klimt. A night and a day and a night on this train: talking, smoking: Afghani *biris* by the window, blowing the green smoke through the bars, into a landscape of red dust and tangled stumps. The occasional blur of a peacock diving off the tracks; blue-green, like taffeta: and then his face: coarse, pocky skin, the roughness of his nose and lips. (The trees were dead.) But full. What he was saying: Afrikaaner-Dutch, Dutch-English: the constant, voluptuous *ya*.

Years later, walking, in the freezing London cold, I went into a Turkish school for immigrants, to warm my hands. I sat on the windowsill in a room high above the canal: looking down, I saw a woman bicycle past, a cello strapped to her back in its black case. It resembled the carapace of an insect about to rupture its shiny skin. I should have seen my future then, in the way that woman carried what she loved along the length of her spine: her home / kept moving.

5. HOW WILL YOU LIVE NOW?

Like this. Brightly. Growing brighter. As the pink ore of Shivalik glows, at dusk. It lasts for five minutes. I have hands: counting always by the three horizontal creases inside each finger. Marking with the thumb. Fourteen. Seconds. He taught me this. How to tell time by my body. Sometimes I want to tell him: I do not understand what you are saying. Instead, I disguise my slowness: asking him, brightly, if he would like another cup of *chai*.

6. HOW WILL YOU LIVE NOW?

I wake in the peristaltic predawn—purple-black, navy-blue, blue—to say good-bye. He drinks some water. Puts his glass down on my bookshelf. Turns.

It takes three days for the remaining water to evaporate. Because it is winter, I don't open the window, and so, for weeks, I breathe in a constantly circulating invisibility. I convince myself such things are true by counting my in-breaths and then counting my out-breaths, per minute, then minutes, then hour. *Om eying hareeng kleeng char moonday ye biche: om eying hareeng kleen—* This goes on until I dream myself as ribs. Four ribs, floating in a body of air. Bird calls. Nausea. The terrifying absence of a stomach, or a throat, or a plastic bucket.

7. WHAT ARE THE CONSEQUENCES OF SILENCE?

Again, nothing. The sky above New York is thick red. I wrote to you but you did not reply. How difficult and corny, checking mail each night. *Nicht.* The paper I wrote on was yellow and clotted with fibres. My nib caught, sometimes, mid-sentence; I wrote:

No, I can't say it. You live somewhere beyond the marrow of / the scarlet, cortical—this. You live somewhere, and there's a dried cream-scum—sea-shore—around the rim of your cup. Which sea? I don't know whether I should face east, or west.

8. WHAT DO YOU REMEMBER ABOUT THE EARTH?

In the absence of Cezannes, I stare at the wavering light world: Venus rising over the hogbacks; the copper striations along the banks of the Colorado river; a waitress's worn stockings; their heels, the light of her body; shop awnings, as seen through Viennese blinds, from a window table. I am trying to keep my heart open. No need to slit the soles of my feet. This is the earth. This is my one jumping life. We began the day in snow. Now the sage. *(How I've missed you.)* A few quick notes, then: To live without fear. South, I open and open. He writes: *you greedy cow.*

9. WHAT ARE THE CONSEQUENCES OF SILENCE?

Harbour. Fresh brown eggs. Curlicue anemones. The songs of whales.

It is difficult to write about love.

Lapsang souchong tea. Smoked chilies. The maps of Utah and New Mexico. Alfalfa bales. And then the cows. A hundred or more: Hereford, Limousine, Brahma. I stare into two hundred eyes at once. We are traveling east, and inland, for the last, or first, time in our lives. I am twenty-five years old.

He writes: *I am thirty-two years old.*

The Tea tastes of bark, and wood-smoke.

You have not written one word about what happened between us.
(In a South African accent.)

The cows cross the river to give birth at the end of each winter. They break the fence, and they swim. I will never eat beef again.

EMILY PECK

Q: Your work shares a sensibility with other chronicles of the grotesque—Katherine Dunn, Flannery O'Connor, Diane Arbus, Nathaniel West. Care to comment on this?

A: More than anything, my writing style is influenced by film and music. I wrote my micro fictions while listening to the *Vertigo* soundtrack by Bernard Herrmann, who also composed scores of other Hitchcock films and several *Twilight Zone* episodes. Listening to film scores really puts me into the world of the film, and writing in a similar tone comes naturally. I really got into Hitchcock films last summer, and I fell in love with the dark psychological themes and intense soundtracks.

⋮

We move together, eternally connected by our tails. My sisters go left while I go right, but we stay in the same place. By the time we figure out how to move as one, we will already have starved.

Every day she mentally replays the moment when she found her son. He was riding the carousel when she spotted him. He was just as she remembered, a happy little boy with blond curls and dimples. As she looked into his bright blue eyes she knew it was John. She only had him for a day until they took him away. The nurses tell her the boy wasn't her son, they say John didn't live past three hours, but she knows they are wrong.

He said aliens abducted him. It was a warm August night back in '45. He said he was asleep for no more than an hour when a loud noise woke him up. Worried about the cattle, he got out of bed and went to check on them, but as he stepped out of his house he was beamed up into a spaceship. The aliens conducted tests on him for two days, but they sent him back to earth unharmed. No one believes his story except for me. I believe him because they abducted me that night too.

I keep a photograph of my parents in a cigar box under my bed. The photo is colorized. I cut it out of a *Photoplay* magazine I stole from a newsstand. I hide it so the sisters don't find it. You can tell I'm their daughter because I look like a carbon-copy of my mother but with my father's dark eyes. My parents fell in love during their second film. When you watch the movie, you can tell they are in love. The way they look at each other is too real to be acting. They were a beautiful couple, but my mother was married when they fell in love. That's why they had to give me up; the scandal would ruin their careers. I'm sure if they knew me they would love me, but they don't answer my letters. I don't think the sisters even send them anymore.

They call me the "Dog Boy of Siberia," but they don't know I'm really from New York. They bought my phony accent that I picked up from my Russian landlord. It's not a good accent, but they've never met a Russian before, so they believe me. I keep to myself. I can't let anyone know my secret. They'd forgive me for being a fake, but if they saw me without the fur they might recognize me. For the past few weeks, my face has been on the front page of newspapers. They call me the "Bronx Butcher."

Sebastian Santos is a legend in his small fishing village of Oyster Bay. He is an old man who speaks broken English and lives on a dilapidated house-boat with his pet ocelot. Some say he is a Spanish pirate hiding from his enemies in Connecticut, others say he was a foreign exchange student in the 50's but was denied re-entry into Mexico because he was arrested for theft. My favorite story is that he is a Guatemalan prince, exiled from his home country. He was in line to be king, but he fell in love with a commoner and was forced choose between his love or his crown. He chose the woman he loved, and built a boat to take her to Portugal, but before they left, she was murdered by his father. Heartbroken, he continued the journey without her. With no experience at sea, and no crew, he ended up in Oyster Bay.

May and June have worked at Kroner's convenience store for the past ten years. I remember the day they came into town, they were all anyone could talk about for weeks. The poor girls were supposed to meet with an agent here, but he never showed up. They've been here ever since. Old man Kroner offered them a job—he figured business would improve with folks wanting to see the girls. It worked for about a month. People would come in to the shop just to look at them or ask them questions. But then we got used to them. Once you get to know them, you see them as two different people, not one person with two heads.

I've taken on some odd jobs. In high school I worked at my uncle's cat taxidermy shop, sweeping up fur and polishing glass eyes. I've coached synchronized swimming at a school for the deaf, tended bar at a vampire-themed dance club, and taught glass blowing at a Mormon sleep-away-camp. But the oddest job I've ever had was the summer I spent as a nanny to two ghost children in Connecticut.

ZARA BELL

Q: Many of your aphorisms seem to be written in response to a painful episode in your life. Do you mind setting the context for these pieces?

A: Most were written shortly after I separated from my husband. It was painful, yes, but ultimately not quite as painful (for me) as staying together—which actually made it even more painful: my wanting something different than what he wanted. We were incompatible in many ways, etc., but our love (whatever that is) has been deeply transformative. I keep thinking of the Leonard Cohen song, *Hallelujah*: Love is not a victory march, it's cold, and it's a broken Hallelujah. But broken is ok because, again, per Cohen (the master aphorist): 'There's a crack in everything, that's how the light gets in.'

⋮

So many years I did this little dance to please someone I didn't want to be with so he wouldn't leave me.

Artificial intelligence is no cure for natural stupidity.

Self-loathing is a kind of luxury; you indulge it if there's a safety net, some-one who loves you—and you hate them for it.

Just because you hate yourself doesn't mean you're not narcissistic.

Young people don't realize that we are all in some stage of decomposition.

What are all the dietary restrictions really about? Gluten-free, low-carb, vegan, paleo, The Zone—as if your possessions and personality were not enough to distinguish you, you use your food to signify your virtues.

The longer I was loyal to him, the more I betrayed myself.

It's eye opening to be without a car: how much I've missed of this scenic city; the satisfaction of arriving at a place when I've used the power of my own body to get me there.

I keep thinking about the items I'd been lugging around in my car before the accident, the things that seemed both of value and a burden. They're gone now, but that's easy. The family I broke when I decided to leave it is not so different—a vessel containing the polar magnetics of giving and getting, having and needing, reaching forth and pulling away. What is a wreck? What is a loss and what a liberation?

There's a sparrow hopping about after crumbs near my table. It cocks its head and seems to eye me. Somehow the silver flash of that little eye—looking for food, watching for safety—reminds me of the cat and dog I just gave up in the separation; I am sad beyond words. I think of the creature comforts of the man I came to resent, the way he stood at the counter to eat his toast, wouldn't sit with his back to the door at restaurants so he'd "have my back." The guilt and grief are almost more than I can bear. And then I think of my own little eye, my own right to safety, dignity, nourishment, freedom, and I just want to die.

Now that it's no longer necessary for me to pretend, I'm not sure what is real.

We'd been together for so long that I walked around as two people, evaluating events according to both of our sensibilities, judging my selves all the while.

I find myself full of all these little events, daily nothings not important enough to tell anyone but him.

I like you so much, I can hardly stand it when you like what I post—but I can't bear it when you don't.

No one is kinder than one who has known cruelty.

Is everyone's opinion as good as everyone else's?

CONTRIBUTORS

LILY AKERMAN lives in New York. Her aphorisms appeared in the previous volume: *Short Flights: Thirty-Two Modern Writers Share Aphorisms of Insight, Imagination, and Wit* (Schaffner Press/2015). Her writing, in longer forms, has been published in *The Stinging Fly, The Pickled Body, The Letters Page,* and *Calyx,* and has been performed at the Dublin Fringe Festival, Cork Midsummer Festival, the Royal Irish Academy of Music, and Princeton's One Act Opera Project. She is a Fulbright scholar.

JOSÉ ANGEL ARAGUZ is a CantoMundo fellow and the author of seven chapbooks as well as the collections *Everything We Think We Hear* (Flori-canto Press/2015) and *Small Fires* (FutureCycle Press/2017). His poems, prose, and reviews have appeared in *Crab Creek Review, Prairie Schooner, The Windward Review,* and *The Bind.* He runs the poetry blog "The Friday Influence" and teaches English and creative writing at Linfield College.

ZARA BELL grew up in Taos, NM. She received her first BFA (Studio Art, 1999) from the University of New Mexico, and her second (Writing, 2016) from The Savannah College of Art and Design. She is currently pursuing an MFA in Painting. She has worked as a personal trainer, massage therapist, freelance writer and jewelry designer, and was, for a short time, an award-winning competitive bodybuilder. Her mixed media work explores identity, corporeality and relational dynamics—topics she also approaches with words. She's fond of aphorisms because they can operate much like pictures: available for instant gratification, trailed by sizable reverberations. Occasionally, when prompted, she speaks of herself in the third-person.

CHARLES BERNSTEIN'S new essay collection is *Pitch of Poetry* (University of Chicago Press/2016). His most recent book of poems is *Recalculating* (University of Chicago Press/2013). In 2010, Farrar, Straus & Giroux published *All the Whiskey in Heaven: Selected Poems.* Bernstein is Donald T. Regan Professor of English and Comparative Literature at the University of Pennsylvania, where he is co-director of PennSound.

JOHN BRADLEY is the author of seven books of poetry and prose, his most recent being *Erotica Atomica* (WordTech/2017). A frequent reviewer of poetry for *Rain Taxi*, he teaches at Northern Illinois University.

ASHLEIGH BRILLIANT is the creator of *POT-SHOTS* and syndicated author of *I May Not Be Totally Perfect, but Parts of Me Are Excellent, and Other Brilliant Thoughts.* 10,000 copyrighted Brilliant Thoughts are available as cards, books etc. He is the world's highest-paid writer (per word).

PATRICK CARR is half of @dogsdoingthings. He studied 20th century literature in graduate school and now works in advertising. He lives in Jersey City, New Jersey with his wife and son.

STEVEN CARTER is a retired emeritus professor of English and former Senior Fulbright Fellow at two Polish universities, having taught for 38 years. He is the recipient of numerous literary awards, including the Schachterle Prize presented by the National Society for Literature and Science, UNESCO's Nuove Lettere International Poetry and Literature

Prize (twice), and The Eric Hoffer Foundation's Montaigne Medal. His work has been translated into Japanese, German, Dutch, and Italian.

S.D. CHROSTOWSKA teaches Humanities and Social & Political Thought at York University in Canada. Among her books is the novel *Permission* (Dalkey Archive Press/2013).

MARGARET CHULA has published eight collections of poetry including, most recently, *Daffodils at Twilight* (Kelsay Books/2017). She has been writing and teaching haiku and Japanese poetic forms for over thirty-five years. Grants from the Oregon Arts Commission and the Regional Arts and Culture Council have supported her work as well as fellowships to the Vermont Studio Center, the Helene Wurlitzer Foundation, and Playa at Summer Lake. Maggie has been a featured speaker and workshop leader at writers' conferences throughout the United States, as well as in Poland, Canada, and Japan. She has also served as president of the Tanka Society of America and as Poet Laureate for Friends of Chamber Music. After living in Kyoto for twelve years, she now makes her home in Portland, Oregon.

LYDIA DAVIS is the author, most recently, of the collection of stories, *Can't and Won't* (Farrar, Straus & Giroux/2014). Her previous works include *Collected Stories* (FSG/2009), a new translation of Flaubert's *Madame Bovary* (Viking Penguin/2010), a chapbook entitled *The Cows* (Sarabande Press/2011), and a long narrative poem entitled "Our Village" in *Two American Scenes* (New Directions/2013). In 2013 she was awarded the Man Booker International Prize for her fiction. She currently serves on the governing board of her village in New York State.

ALAIN DE BOTTON was born in 1969 and is the author of 15 books of fiction and non-fiction including *How Proust can Change Your Life* (Vintage/1998), and *The Course of Love* (Simon & Schuster/2017). In 2008 he founded The School of Life (www.theschooloflife.com); an institution devoted to emotional education.

CHARLENE DEGUZMAN is a writer and actress who first garnered attention for tweeting her self-deprecating thoughts as @charstarlene. She was named one of the funniest people on Twitter by *Rolling Stone, Playboy, The Huffington Post, Buzzfeed, Funny Or Die*, and more. She went on to write and star in numerous short films on YouTube. Her most popular film, *I Forgot My Phone*, has over 50 million views and was featured in *The New York Times, USA Today, Time, NPR, Fox News, Good Morning America, Vice, The Today Show*, and more. In 2016, with the help of indie film hero Mark Duplass, she crowdfunded her first feature film, *Unlovable*, in which she stars with John Hawkes and Melissa Leo. Charlene's intention for the rest of her life is to help people feel understood and less alone through all of her creative adventures. www.charstarlene.com

FRANK DIXON loved to read fairy tales as a child. From the time he was 7 he was writing his own stories and drawing pictures to go with them. At age 14 he created words and images for an original 460-page adventure story about flying saucers, a volcano, and a giant. Dixon studied art and illustration at Art Center College of Design and received his MFA in fine arts from California State University at Los Angeles. His background ranges from portrait artist on the Queen Mary, to award-winning graphic designer/illustrator for NASA, to a popular art instructor in Southern California. He teaches drawing, painting, and illustration at Quartz Hill High School and Antelope Valley College.

STEPHEN DOBYNS has published fourteen books of poems, twenty-three novels, a book of short stories, and two books of essays on poetry. His most recent book of poems is *The Day's Last Light Reddens the Leaves of the Copper Beech* (BOA Editions Ltd./2016). His most recent novel is *Saratoga Payback* (Blue Rider Press/2017). Two of Dobyns' novels and two of his short stories have been made into films. His book of poems *Black Dog, Red Dog* (Carnegie-Mellon University Press/1997) was made into a feature length film in 2015 by James Franco. He has received a Guggenheim fellowship, three fellowships from the National Endowment for the Arts and numerous prizes for his poetry and fiction. Dobyns teaches in the MFA Program of Warren Wilson College, and in the past he has taught at Sarah Lawrence College, Emerson College, Syracuse University, Boston University, University of Iowa and more. He was born in Orange, New Jersey in 1941. He lives in Westerly, RI.

SHARON DOLIN is the author of six poetry collections, most recently *Manual for Living* (University of Pittsburgh Press/2016) and *Whirlwind* (University of Pittsburgh Press/2012). Her other recent books include: *Serious Pink* (Marsh Hawk Press/2015) and *Burn and Dodge* (University of Pittsburgh Press/2008), which won the AWP Donald Hall Prize for Poetry. Her aphoristic sequences have appeared in such journals as *Denver Quarterly*, *Fourth Genre*, *Hotel Amerika*, *The Kenyon Review online*, the *Seneca Review*, and *Terrain*. Among her recent honors, she received a Witter Bynner Fellowship from the Library of Congress and a PEN/Heim Translation Fund grant. She lives and teaches in New York City and directs Writing About Art in Barcelona each June. http://www.sharon-dolin.com/barcelona-workshops/

OLIVIA DRESHER is a publisher, editor, anthologist, and writer of poetic fragments & aphorisms. Her poetry, fragments, and essays have appeared in anthologies and a variety of online and print literary magazines. She is the editor of *In Pieces: An Anthology of Fragmentary Writing* (Impassio Press/2006) and co-editor of the anthology *Darkness and Light: Private Writing as Art* (iUniverse/2000). She has spontaneously tweeted thousands of fragments & aphorisms on Twitter, where she has a large following, and plans to choose some of these for several in-print collections. Her complete bio and select writings can be found at OliviaDresher.com.

THOMAS FARBER has been a Fulbright Scholar, as well as a recipient of the Dorothea Lange-Paul Taylor Prize, a Guggenheim, a Rockefeller Foundation scholar at Bellagio, and three National Endowment fellowships for fiction and non-fiction. His recent books include *Here And Gone* (El Leon Literary Arts/2015), *The End of My Wits* (El Leon Literary Arts/2015), *Brief Nudity* (El Leon Literary Arts/2009), and *The Beholder*

(Metropolitan Books/2002). Former Visiting Distinguished Writer at the University of Hawai'i, he teaches at the University of California, Berkeley, and is Publisher/Editor-in-Chief of El León Literary Arts. visit www. thomasfarber.org

SAMI FEIRING (born 1963) is a Finnish aphorist living in Helsinki. He has studied international politics at the Helsinki University and is a founding member of the World Aphorism Organization. He was the president of the Aphorism Association of Finland from 2005 till 2012. He teaches the art of writing aphorisms and has also edited and written several books on the subject, including an anthology of Finnish aphorisms *Tiheiden ajatusten kirja*, (2011) and a handbook on the art of aphorism *Lyhyesti sanomisen taide* (2014).

ISAAC FELLOWS lives with his family in Portland, Oregon, where he works as a children's librarian. Most of his writing never gets written down.

ELISA GABBERT, a poet and essayist, is the author of three collections: *L'Heure Bleue, or the Judy Poems* (Black Ocean/2016), *The Self Unstable* (Black Ocean/2013), and *The French Exit* (Birds LLC/2010). Her work has appeared in The *New Yorker, Boston Review, Pacific Standard, Guernica, The Awl, Electric Literature, Harvard Review, The Threepenny Review,* and in anthologies including *The Manifesto Project* (University of Akron Press/2017), *Privacy Policy: The Anthology of Surveillance Poetics* (Black Ocean/2014), *The Book of Scented Things: 100 Contemporary Poems About Perfume* (Literary House Press/2014), and *The Monkey and the Wrench: Essays into Contemporary Poetics* (University of Akron Press/2011). She lives in Denver. Learn more at elisagabbert.com

MIKE GINN is one of several comedy writers living in Los Angeles. He hails from the Pacific Northwest and hopes to be buried there someday soon.

GEMMA GORGA was born and lives in Barcelona, Spain, where she is Professor of Medieval and Renaissance Spanish Literature. She has published six collections of poetry. The aphoristic prose poems are from *Llibre dels minuts* (*Book of Minutes*, Barcelona, 2006), which won the Premi Miquel de Palol (2006). A bilingual edition of *Book of Minutes*, translated by Sharon Dolin, is forthcoming from the Field Translation Series (Oberlin University Press) in 2019.

KEVIN GRIFFITH, who teaches at Capital University, in Columbus, OH, is the author of many books, including a collection of prose poetry, *Denmark, Kangaroo, Orange* (Pearl Editions/2008), and a collection of micro-fiction, *101 Kinds of Irony* (Folded Word/2012). He has been awarded three Ohio Arts Council Fellowships for Excellence in Poetry, the most recent being in 2014. He and his son recently launched the website Brickjest.com, which recreates David Foster Wallace's 1,079 page novel *Infinite Jest* entirely in Legos.

DR. MARDY GROTHE is a retired psychologist, management consultant, and platform speaker. He is the author of seven "word and language" books, including *Oxymoronica* (Harper/2004), *I Never Metaphor I Didn't Like* (Harper/2008), *Viva la Repartee* (Harper/2005), and, most recently *Metaphors Be With You* (Harper/2016). He is also the creator of "Dr. Mardy's Dictionary of Metaphorical Quotations" (DMDMQ), the world's largest online database of metaphorical quotations. He lives in Southern Pines, North Carolina, with his wife, Katherine Robinson. Website: www.drmardy.com

JAMES GUIDA was born in Philadelphia in 1978 and grew up in Canberra, Australia. His collection of aphorisms *Marbles* came out in 2009 from Turtle Point Press, while essays and reviews on a range of cultural subjects can be found at the websites for *The New Yorker* and *The New York Review of Books*. www.jamesguida.com

AARON HASPEL is the author of *Everything: A Book of Aphorisms* (Good Books/2015). He lives in New York.

JOY HARJO is a member of the Mvskoke Nation. Her most recent collection of poetry is *Conflict Resolution for Holy Beings* (W.W. Norton & Company/2017). She has written a memoir, *Crazy Brave* (W.W. Norton & Company/2013), children's books, and is at work on a new album of music and a play that will restore southeastern natives to the origin story of blues and jazz.

DENISE HAYES was born in Yorkshire, England. She studied at Birmingham University in the UK and was a university lecturer in Creative Writing for many years but is now old enough to have the freedom to write full time. Denise's poems have appeared in various magazines including *New Poetry*, *Mslexia*, *Glitterwolf*, and *Hearing Voices*. Denise's flash fiction and short stories have been anthologized in collections such as the prize-winning Anthology, *Overheard: Stories to Read Aloud* (Salt/2012), *Fusion* (Fantastic Books/2012) and *666* (Fantastic Books/2016). She has a particular interest in aphorisms and has presented conference papers and published academic articles on the Spanish Gregueria—a quirky form made famous by Ramón Gómez de la Serna. She tweets on Ramón's Gregueria, Old Norse proverbs, and more recent pithy tidbits on her Twitter page @Gregueria1. She lives in rural seclusion in a rose-covered cottage in Worcestershire.

JANE HIRSHFIELD is the author of eight much-honored books of poetry and six collections of essays, co-translations, and anthologies, most recently *The Beauty* (Knopf/2015), long-listed for the 2015 National Book Award in Poetry, and *Ten Windows: How Great Poems Transform the World* (Knopf/2015), winner of the Northern California Book Award. Her other honors include fellowships from the NEA, The Guggenheim and Rockefeller Foundations, the California Book Award, and the Donald Hall-Jane Kenyon Award. Her work has appeared in *The New Yorker*, *The Atlantic*, *The New York Review of Books*, *Poetry*, *The Paris Review*, *The Guardian*, and eight editions of *The Best American Poems*. In 2012 she was elected a Chancellor of the Academy of American Poets.

H. L. HIX'S recent books include two poetry collections, *Rain Inscription* (Etruscan Press/2017), and *American Anger* (Etruscan Press/2016), and an art/poetry anthology, *Ley Lines* (Wilfrid Laurier Univ. Press/2014). He is a professor and former director of the creative writing MFA program at the University of Wyoming. His website is www.hlhix.com.

Once a young and promising Ivy-League professor of German, **ERIC JAROSINSKI** has gone on to find his true calling as a failed and former Ivy-League professor of German. He is currently the editor and sole author of @NeinQuarterly, the world's leading fictitious journal of utopian negation, and a columnist for the German weekly *Die Zeit*. Jarosinski regularly takes his stand-up philosophy/sit-down comedy on the road internationally as part of his ongoing Failed Intellectual Goodwill Tour. His first book, *Nein. A Manifesto* (Grove Press, Black Cat/2015), has been published in six languages.

KARL JIRGENS, former Head of the English Department at the University of Windsor, is the author of four books (Coach House, Mercury, and ECW Presses). He edited two books, one on painter Jack Bush and another on poet Christopher Dewdney, as well as an issue of *Open Letter* magazine (featuring contemporary literary theory). His scholarly and creative pieces are published globally. His research on digital media investigates literature and performance. From 1979 to 2016, Jirgens edited *Rampike,* an international journal featuring contemporary art, writing, and theory. He currently serves as a Professor with the English Department at the University of Windsor (Canada).

BHANU KAPIL is the author of five books: *The Vertical Interrogation of Strangers* (Kelsey Street Press), *Incubation: A Space For Monsters* (Kelsey Street Press/2001), *Humanimal: A Project For Future Children* (Kelsey Street Press/2009), *Schizophrene* (Nightboat Books/2011) and *Ban en Banlieue* (Nightboat/2015).

IRENA KARAFILLY is an award-winning Montreal writer, poet, and aphorist. She is the author of several acclaimed books and of numerous stories, poems, and articles, which have been published in both literary and consumer magazines, as well as in various North American newspapers, including *The New York Times* and the *International Herald Tribune*. Some of her short stories have been anthologized and/or broadcast, winning literary prizes such as the National Magazine Award and the CBC Literary Award. Her latest novel, *The House on Selkirk Avenue* (Guernica/2017), has recently been released in Canada. For more information, please visit: irenakarafilly.com

KARL KEMPTON lives happily with his beloved wife Ruth in Oceano, California. He relocated to the beautiful central coast in 1975. His lexical & visual poems have been published internationally in 45 titles, 50 anthologies and seen in numerous group exhibitions since the early 1970s. He edited and published the international journal of visual poetry, *Kaldron*, from 1976 to 1991, and conceived and cofounded the ongoing poetry festival in San Luis Obispo in 1983. His environmental activism includes working for and with the Chumash people, stopping agricultural pesticide spraying and ocean protection currently in the hands of a committee pursuing national marine sanctuary status http://chumashsanctuary.com. His latest book is *poems about something & nothing* (Paper Press/2015). He is currently writing a book on the history of visual text arts.

Individual entries on **RICHARD KOSTELANETZ'S** work in several fields appear in various editions of
Wikipedia
NNDB.com
Britannica.com
Postmodern Fiction
Contemporary Poets
Who's Who in America
Contemporary Novelists

Who's Who in the World
Who's Who in American Art
Directory of American Scholars
Advocates for Self-Government
The Chronology of American Literature
The Facts on File Companion to American Poetry
Merriam-Webster's Dictionary of American Writers
Contemporary Jewish-American Dramatists and Poets
Baker's Biographical Dictionary of Musicians
Readers Guide to Twentieth-Century Writers
Who's Who in U.S. Writers, Editors, and Poets
The Merriam-Webster Encyclopedia of Literature
International Who's Who of Authors and Writers
The Facts on File Companion to 20th Century Poetry
The HarperCollins Reader's Encyclopedia of American Literature
The Greenwood Encyclopedia of Multiethnic American Literature
The Greenwood Encyclopedia of American Poets and Poetry
Honor Wall of Distinguished Alumni, Scarsdale High School, NY

YAHIA LABABIDI, Egyptian-American, is the author of 7 books of poetry and prose. Lababidi's latest book, *Where Epics Fail* (Unbound/Penguin Random House, 2018), is a collection of 800 new aphorisms which was featured on PBS NewsHour and generously endorsed by Richard Blanco, Barack Obama's inaugural poet. *Epics* is available for order here: https://unbound.com/books/where-epics-fail. Lababidi's work has also appeared on NPR, *Best American Poetry*, *AGNI*, *World Literature Today*, *On Being with Krista Tippett* and he has participated in international poetry festivals throughout the USA, Eastern Europe as well as the Middle East. Twice nominated for a Pushcart Prize, Lababidi's writing has been translated into Arabic, Hebrew, Slovak, Spanish, French, Italian, German, Dutch, and Swedish.

CLAYTON LAMAR is a writer, editor, and half of @dogsdoingthings. He writes (and reads) science fiction, poetry, and other occasional forms. He studied at NYU and Rutgers and works in university education. He lives in New York.

LANCE LARSEN, who recently completed a five-year appointment as Utah's Poet Laureate, is the author of five poetry collections, most recently *What the Body Knows* (Tampa/2018). His prose and poetry appear widely, in such venues as *Southern Review, TLS, APR, Poetry, River Styx, Georgia Review, Brevity*, and *Best American Poetry 2009*. He has received a number of awards, including a Pushcart Prize and an NEA fellowship. The pieces included herein are excerpted from a manuscript titled *APHORISMS FOR A LONELY PLANET*. In the summer he will direct a theater study abroad program in London.

DAVID LAZAR was a Guggenheim Fellow in Nonfiction for 2015-16. His books include *Who's Afraid of Helen of Troy?: An Essay on Love (Etruscan Press/2016)*, *After Montaigne* (University of Georgia Press/2013), *Occasional Desire: Essays* (University of Nebraska Press/2013), *The Body of Brooklyn* (University of Iowa Press/2013), *Truth in Nonfiction* (University of Iowa Press/2008), *Essaying the Essay* (Welcome Table Press/2014), *Powder Town* (Pecan Grove Press/2008), *Michael Powell: Interviews* (University Press of Mississippi/2003), and *Conversations with M.F.K. Fisher* (University Press of Mississippi/1992). Forthcoming from the University of Nebraska Press are *I'll Be Your Mirror: Essays and Aphorisms*, in 2017, and *Characters*. Seven of his essays have been "Notable Essays of the Year" according to *Best American Essays*. Lazar created the Ph.D. program in nonfiction writing at Ohio University and directed the creation of the undergraduate and M.F.A. programs in Nonfiction Writing at Columbia College, Chicago where he is Professor of Creative Writing. He is founding editor of the literary magazine *Hotel Amerika*, now in its seventeenth year, and series editor, with Patrick Madden, of *21ˢᵗ Century Essays*, at Ohio State University Press.

DAN LIEBERT is in his sixties and has been working in 'short forms' of written expression since his early teens. This included aphorisms, greguerias, haiku, senryu, Sanskrit style rasa-ananda (mood/bliss) poems, prose poems and even for a time stand-up comedy.

JAMES LOUGH'S most recent book is *Short Flights: Thirty-Two Modern Writers Share Aphorisms of Insight, Imagination, and Wit* (Schaffner Press/2015). His oral history, *This Ain't No Holiday Inn: Down and Out in New York's Chelsea Hotel 1980-1995* (SchaffnerPress/2013) has been optioned by Lionsgate Entertainment for TV production. His collection of nature essays, *Sites of Insight* (University Press of Chicage/2003) won the Colorado Endowment for the Humanities Publications Prize. *Spheres of Awareness: A Wilberian Integral Approach to Literature, Philosophy, Psychology, and Art* (UPA/2009) features philosophical and spiritual essays based on the integral philosophy of Ken Wilber. He has published over 80 articles, essays, and short stories, and served as an editor with *ArtPULSE* magazine, *The Denver Quarterly*, *Divide*, *Bastard Review*, *Document*, and *Artemis*. He is a professor of nonfiction writing in the Savannah College of Art and Design's writing department, which he formerly directed. Lough is a 2017 winner of *Electric Literature*'s 280-Character Story Contest.

SARAH MANGUSO is the author of the nonfiction books *300 Arguments: Essays* (Graywolf/2017), *Ongoingness: The End of a Diary* (Graywolf/2016), *The Guardians: An Elegy for a Friend* (Picador/2013), and *The Two Kinds of Decay: A Memoir* (Picador/2009); the story collection *Hard to Admit and Harder to Escape* (McSweeney's/2007); and the poetry collections *Siste Viator* (Four Way/2006) and *The Captain Lands in Paradise* (Alice James Books/2002). Her work has been supported by a Guggenheim Fellowship, a Hodder Fellowship, and the Rome Prize, and her books have been translated into five languages. Her poems have won a Pushcart Prize and appeared in four editions of the *Best American Poetry* series, and her essays regularly appear in such venues as *Harper's*, *McSweeney's*, the *New York Times*, and the *Paris Review*. She has taught at Princeton, Columbia, the Pratt Institute, the Otis College of Art and Design, and many other institutions, and held the Mary Routt Chair of Creative Writing at Scripps College. She lives in Los Angeles and currently teaches at CalArts.

MICHAEL MARTONE was born in Fort Wayne, Indiana. He has taught at several universities including Johns Hopkins, Iowa State, Harvard, Alabama, and Syracuse. He participated in the last major memo war fought with actual paper memoranda before the advent of electronic email. Staples were deployed. The paper generated in that war stacks several inches deep, thick enough to stop a bullet. Martone learned that the "cc:" is the most strategic field of the memo's template, and he is sad to realize that fewer and fewer readers know what the "cc:" stands for let alone have ever held a piece of the delicate and duplicating artifact in their ink stained and smudge smudged fingers. It, like everything else, is history.

DINTY W. MOORE is author of *The Story Cure: A Book Doctor's Pain-Free Guide to Finishing Your Novel or Memoir* (Ten Speed Press/2017), the memoir *Between Panic & Desire* (Bison Books/2010), and many other books. He has published essays and stories in *The Southern Review*, *The Georgia Review*, *Harpers*, *The New York Times Sunday Magazine*, *Arts & Letters*, *The Normal School*, and elsewhere. Moore has won many awards for his writing, including a National Endowment for the Arts Fellowship in Fiction. He edits *Brevity*, an online journal of flash nonfiction, and lives in Athens, Ohio, where he grows heirloom tomatoes and edible dandelions.

GEORGE MURRAY is the author of two bestselling collections of aphorisms, *Glimpse* (ECW Press/2010) and *Quick* (ECW/2017). He is also the author of seven books of poetry and one book for children. His work appears widely in anthologies, as well as international magazines and journals such as *Granta*, *Hotel Amerika*, *Iowa Review*, *London Magazine*, *New American Writing*, *New Welsh Review*, *The Walrus*, etc. He lives in St. John's, Newfoundland.

ERIC NELSON lives in Asheville, North Carolina, and teaches in UNC-Asheville's Great Smokies Writing Program. His sixth poetry collection is *Some Wonder* (Gival Press/2015). His poems have appeared in *Poetry*, *The Sun*, *The Oxford American*, *Poetry Daily*, *Verse Daily*, and many other venues.

MAGGIE NELSON is the author of nine books of poetry and prose, many of which have become cult classics defying categorization. Her nonfiction titles include the *New York Times* bestseller and National Book Critics Circle Award winner *The Argonauts* (Graywolf/2015), *The Art of Cruelty: A Reckoning* (W.W. Norton & Company/2011), a *New York Times* Notable Book of the Year, *Bluets* (Wave Books/2009), named by Bookforum as one of the top 10 best books of the past 20 years, *The Red Parts* (Free Press/2007), reissued 2016, and *Women, the New York School, and Other True Abstractions* (University of Iowa Press/2007). Her poetry titles include *Something Bright, Then Holes* (Soft Skull Press/2007) and *Jane: A Murder* (Soft Skull Press/2005), finalist for the PEN/Martha Albrand Art of the Memoir. She has been the recipient of a Guggenheim Fellowship in Nonfiction, an NEA in Poetry, an Innovative Literature Fellowship from Creative Capital, and an Arts Writers Fellowship from the Andy Warhol Foundation. In 2016 she was awarded a MacArthur "genius" Fellowship. She is currently on the faculty of USC and lives in Los Angeles.

WILLIAM PANNAPACKER, DuMez Professor of English at Hope College in Holland, Michigan, has a Ph.D. in American Civilization from Harvard, and is the author of numerous scholarly publications on literature and history. He also was a columnist for *The Chronicle of Higher Education* from 1998 to 2014 and has contributed to *The New York Times* and *Slate*. Twertzog's tweets for 2016 were selected for *The Best American Nonrequired Reading 2017* edited by Sarah Vowell.

DON PATERSON is a poet, editor and musician; he is Professor of Poetry at the University of St Andrews, and Poetry Editor at Picador Macmillan. He lives in Edinburgh, Scotland. His most recent collection of poetry is *40 Sonnets* (Farrar, Straus and Giroux/2017). He has published two collections of aphorisms, *The Book of Shadows* (Picador/2004) and *The Blind Eye* (Faber/ 2007) and a compendium, *Best Thought, Worst Thought* (Graywolf/ 2008). A new collection will appear in 2018.

EMILY PECK graduated from the Savannah College of Art and Design with an MFA in Themed Entertainment Design in 2017. With a background in film and theater, she is currently building a career designing immersive storytelling experiences.

MEG POKRASS has published stories in *McSweeney's, Gigantic, RATTLE, Five Points, Wigleaf, Smokelong,* and numerous other literary magazines online and in print. Her work has been internationally anthologized, most recently in the Norton anthology *Flash Fiction International* (W.W. Norton & Company/2015) and the forthcoming anthology *New Micro-fiction* (W.W. Norton & Company/2018*).* Meg received the *Blue Light Book Award* for her collection of prose poetry, *Cellulose Pajamas* (Blue Light Press/2016). Her other collections include *Damn Sure Right* (Press 53/2011), *My Very End of the Universe* (Rose Metal Press/2014), *Bird Envy* (Harvard Book Store/2014) and *The Dog Looks Happy Upside Down* (Etruscan Press/2016). She is the flash fiction curator for Great Jones Street App, and curates the Bath Flash Fiction Festival (Bath, U.K.). You can learn more at megpokrass.com

HART POMERANTZ is a Canadian lawyer and television personality, best known for his collaboration with *Saturday Night Live* producer Lorne Michaels in *The Hart and Lorne Terrific Hour*. However, Pomerantz is also well known to Canadian audiences through his many appearances as a regular on *This Is the Law*, where he brought a unique sense of irreverent humor to the show along with his legal knowledge. More recently, he was the host of the short-lived Prime series *Grumps*. He is a graduate of the University of Toronto Law School and currently resides in Toronto, Ontario.

PAUL LOBO PORTUGÉS taught creative writing at UCSB, UC Berkeley, USC, SBCC, Cuesta College, and the University of Provence. His books include *Sorrow and Hope* (Finishing Line Press/2016), *Breaking Bread* (Finishing Line Press/2013), and *Ginsberg: On Tibetan Buddhism, Mantras, and Drugs* (World Temple Press/2013). His poems are scattered in small magazines (*Hambone, Chelsea, River Styx*) and anthologies *(El Tecolote, Overthrowing Capitalism, The Asian Writer, Naropa Anthology, Spectrum—So Cal Poets Anthology)*, across the Americas, Europe, Latin America, and Asia. He has written films, including *The Look of Love, Behind the Veil, Shakespeare's Last Bed, Fire From the Mountain*. His videos of poetry include *To My Beloved, Kiss, The Lonely Wind, Lovers, Of Her I Sing, Fathermine, Stones from Heaven, The Killing Fields of Darfur, Who on Earth*. He has recieved awards from the National Endowment, the Ford Foundation, and the Fulbright Commission.

CLAUDIA RANKINE is the author of five collections of poetry, including *Citizen: An American Lyric* (Graywolf Press/2014), and *Don't Let Me Be Lonely* (Graywolf Press/2004); two plays, including *Provenance of Beauty: A South Bronx Travelogue*; numerous video collaborations, and is the editor of several anthologies including *The Racial Imaginary: Writers on Race in the Life of the Mind* (Fence Books/2015). Among her numerous awards and honors, Rankine is the recipient of the Bobbitt National Prize for Poetry, the Poets & Writers' Jackson Poetry Prize, and fellowships from the Guggenheim Foundation, the Lannan Foundation, the MacArthur Foundation, United States Artists, and the National Endowment of the Arts. She is a Chancellor of the Academy of American Poets and teaches at Yale University as the Frederick Iseman Professor of Poetry.

JAMES RICHARDSON'S aphorisms and microlyrics can be found in *During* (Copper Canyon Press/2016), *By the Numbers* (Copper Canyon Press/2010), a National Book Award finalist, *Interglacial: New and Selected Poems and Aphorisms* (Ausable Press/2004), a National Book Critics Circle Award finalist, and *Vectors: Aphorisms & Ten-Second Essays* (Ausable Press/2001).

MARTY RUBIN is an aphorist/philosopher and bum/happiness freak. His blog is at wwwaphorismscom.blogspot.com. He lives in New York.

ANA MARÍA SHUA (Buenos Aires, 1951) has earned a prominent place in Argentinian fiction with publications in nearly every genre: poetry, microfiction, short stories, novels, children's fiction, books of humor and Jewish folklore, anthologies, journalistic articles, and essays. Her works have garnered national and international awards and have been translated into more than a dozen languages. Her novels include *Soy Paciente* (1980), *Los amores de Laurita* (1984), *El libro de los recuerdos* (1994, Guggenheim Fellowship), *La muerte como efecto secundario* (1997), *El peso de la tentación* (2007), and *Hija* (2016), and some have been adapted to movies and plays. Her first four books of microfiction were published in one volume *Cazadores de Letras* (2009), followed by another book of microfiction, *Fenómenos de circo* (2011). Her four books of short stories were published in one volume *Que tengas una vida interesante* (2009), followed by a new collection *Contra el tiempo* (2013). All five of her books of microfictions have been published in the anthology *Todos los universos posibles* (2017).

CHARLES SIMIC is a Serbian-American poet and co-Poetry editor of The *Paris Review*. In 2007, he was appointed the 15th Poet Laureate Consultant in Poetry to the Library of Congress. He has published twenty-eight books, and his book of prose poems, *The World Doesn't End* (Harvest Books/1989) won the 1990 Pulitzer Prize. He won a MacArthur Fellowship in 1984, the Wallace Stevens award in 2007, and the Griffin Poetry Prize in 2004.

AUSTIN SMITH'S poems have appeared in *The New Yorker*, *POETRY*, *Threepenny Review*, *Yale Review*, *Sewanee Review*, *Hopkins Review* and *ZYZZYVA*, amongst others. His first poetry collection, *Almanac: Poems* (Princeton University Press/2013), was selected by Paul Muldoon for the Princeton Series of Contemporary Poets. He lives in Oakland, CA and teaches at Stanford University.

BRIAN JAY STANLEY'S essays have been published in *The New York Times*, *Pleiades*, *The Antioch Review*, *North American Review*, *The Sun*, *The Hudson Review*, and elsewhere. They were selected as notable essays in *The Best American Essays* in 2006, 2010, 2011, 2013, 2014, and 2015, and have been anthologized in *America Now*, 9th ed. (Bedford/St. Martin's Press/2011). He lives in Asheville, North Carolina. More of his writing can be found on his website, www.brianjaystanley.com.

ALEX STEIN is the co-editor, with James Lough, of *Short Flights: 32 Modern Writers Share Aphorisms of Insight Inspiration and Wit* (Schaffner Press/2015). His other books include *Weird Emptiness: Essays and Aphorisms* (Wings Press/2007), and *Dark Optimism* (Emerson's Eye Press/1999). He works in the George C. Norlin Library at the University of Colorado ("Enter Here The Timeless Fellowship Of The Human Spirit") and holds a Ph.D. from the University of Denver. He is at home in Boulder, CO.

MICHAEL THEUNE is Professor of English and Writing Program Director at Illinois Wesleyan University in Bloomington, Illinois. He edited *Structure & Surprise: Engaging Poetic Turns* (Teachers & Writers/2007), co-edited *Voltage Poetry* (voltagepoetry.com), and co-authored *We Need to Talk: A New Method for Evaluating Poetry* (Multilingual Matters/2017). Theune's poetry and criticism have appeared in numerous publications, including journals such as *Alaska Quarterly Review*, *American Poet: The Journal of the Academy of American Poets*, *College English*, *The Iowa Review*, *The New Republic*, and *Pleiades*, and essay collections such as *Creative Writing and Education* (Multilingual Matters/2014), *Beyond the Workshop: Creative Writing, Theory & Practice* (Kingston UP/2012), and *Mentor and Muse: Essays from Poets to Poets* (Southern Illinois UP/2010). He is a founding editor of the Keats Letters Project (keatslettersproject.com).

HOLLY WOODWARD is a writer and painter. A book of poems, *Sin for Beginners*, was finalist for the National Poetry Series. She is on Twitter, where her avatar is an owl, which doesn't tweet.

never never never never never never never always never never never never never never never
never never never never never never never always never never never never never never never
never never never never never never never always never never never never never never never
never never never never never never never always never never never never never never never
never never never never never never never always never never never never never never never
never never never never never never never always never never never never never never never
never never never never never never never always never never never never never never never
never never never never never never never always never never never never never never never
never never never never never never never always never never never never never never never
never never never never never never never always never never never never never never never
never never never never never never never always never never never never never never never
never never never never never never never always never never never never never never never
never never never never never never never always never never never never never never never
never never never never never never never always never never never never never never never
never never never never never never never always never never never never never never never
never never never never never never never always never never never never never never never
never never never never never never never always never never never never never never never
never never never never never never never always never never never never never never never
never never never never never never never always never never never never never never never
never never never never never never never always never never never never never never never
never never never never never never never always never never never never never never never
never never never never never never never always never never never never never never never
never never never never never never never always never never never never never never never
never never never never never never never always never never never never never never never
always always always always always always always always always always always always al
lways always always always always always now always always always always always alway
always always always always always always always always always always always always al
never never never never never nevernever always never never never never never never never
never never never never never never never always never never never never never never neve
never never never never never never never always never never never never never never never
never never never never never never never always never never never never never never never
never never never never never never never always never never never never never never never
never never never never never never never always never never never never never never never
never never never never never never never always never never never never never never never
never never never never never never never always never never never never never never never
never never never never never never never always never never never never never never never
never never never never never never never always never never never never never never never
never never never never never never never always never never never never never never never
never never never never never never never always never never never never never never never
never never never never never never never always never never never never never never never
never never never never never never never always never never never never never never never
never never never never never never never always never never never never never never never
never never never never never never never always never never never never never never never
never never never never never never never always never never never never never never never
never never never never never never never always never never never never never never never
never never never never never never never always never never never never never never never
never never never never never never never always never never never never never never never
never never never never never never never always never never never never never never never
never never never never never never never always never never never never never never never
never never never never never never never never always never never never never never never never